Prague Shopping Guide:
From Trinkets to Treasures

KRYSTI BRICE

ALSO BY KRYSTI BRICE:

ISBN: 198618028X
ISBN-13: 978-1986180283

DEDICATION

This Prague Shopping Guide is dedicated to my sister Stephanie, the ultimate shopper, who taught me that shopping can be both artful and fun.

CONTENTS

ACKNOWLEDGMENTS

Heartfelt thanks go out to Julie, who helped me in gathering the information for this book, and to Marjanka for helping to ensure the accuracy of the information contained herein.

1 INTRODUCTION

Since the Velvet Revolution of 1989, Prague has been undergoing a transformation in all areas of life. And probably in no other area (well, other than dining) has it gone through a bigger change than in the area of – you guessed it – shopping! When I arrived here in 1992, a roll of toilet paper wasn't easy to come by. To be sure, there was enough of it around, but only a few shops had it, and the shop hours were such that I had to take a break from work before the shop closest to my office closed if I wanted to be sure I had some on hand (and there was only one kind: brown). And as I mention in my Prague restaurant guide, orange juice simply didn't exist, and neither did a lot of seemingly "ordinary" things that I had come to take for granted having grown up in the US.

Shop windows in those days varied from amusing to depressing to deceptive: often the best items in a shop's possession were those on display in the windows; once you ventured into the store to buy whatever item you wanted that you had seen in the window, however, you were quickly disappointed when you found out that it wasn't for sale in the store. It was on display only in the window because… why not?

That phenomenon might be the source of the all-too-common refrain you heard in Czech stores in those days when you asked for a particular item that happened to be out of stock: "Nejsou." For

1

example: "Do you have pantyhose?" might generate the following reply from the shop assistant: "Oni *nejsou.*" That answer in Czech means that *they don't exist* (literally, "*they aren't*"). So, rather than, "Nemáme" – "we don't have" or "we're out" – you were told that what you want doesn't exist. This always struck me as odd. "Surely you mean that you don't *have* them, but they *do* exist, don't they?" I thought. Even in large department stores where a greater supply of items was normally available, if an item was out the wording of the reply to "Do you have...?" was always "*nejsou*" – they don't exist rather than "we're out (at the moment)," or "we don't have (carry) them" – now or ever. Even when you had previously purchased the item in question in said store, this was the answer you got! You were told that they didn't exist even when you knew they had previously been in the store!

After enough time in Prague and enough experience with what was still a very communist-like world in look and feel I surmised that this reply was most likely the result of the fact that under communism, some things simply weren't available. Or, even if they had been available at one time, they might not ever be again. It was still that way for a number of years after I moved to Prague in 1992. So for all intents and purposes, something that was not in stock in the shop did not exist in the Czech world. Why complicate things by implying that they might one day "exist"? Interestingly, now that Prague has just about everything available for sale, the phrase "oni nejsou" has disappeared from the shopping lexicon entirely. You never hear it anymore, I'm happy to say. And if something happens to not be available in a shop, you'll be told, "nemáme."

Another common refrain in the early days (which does not necessarily relate to shopping, but which I'll share anyway) was "není možné," which means, "it's not possible." Let's say you went to a restaurant with three friends and you encountered only tables for two. So, logically you would ask the waiter, "May we push these two tables next to each other so that we can sit together?" "*To není možné,*" ("it's not possible"), the waiter would reply. "Není možné" was usually preceded by "Bohužel," a word meaning "unfortunately" whose etymology includes the root for the word "God" and basically means "We tried everything, even with God's help, and still we were not successful." In my logical mind, as with "nejsou," I'd say to myself, "I think you mean that it's *possible*, but you just won't do it." And the expat community at the time often joked that "bohužel" was the most common word in the Czech language.

The frequency of hearing "není možné" nearly drove a French colleague of mine at Deloitte mad and led him to constantly proclaim in frustration after each disappointment or setback: "Czechoslovakia, the country where everything is doable but nothing is possible." A Parisian through and through, he had been sent to Prague as a substitute (punishment?) for otherwise losing his job to downsizing in the Paris office had he remained in France, and he suffered terribly from Prague's lack of good wine and, as he put it, "nice, smelly cheese" in the early days following the Velvet Revolution. Sadly, he no longer lives here, but he would certainly fare better in the city now if he did.

On the downside, some desirable aspects of the old shopping scene have left (truly, oni nejsou). Examples are packages expertly wrapped in plain paper without the use of tape in lieu (due to the absence) of a shopping bag; quaint little bookshops; almost all of the "antikvariáts" (shops with old maps, books and prints) that used to litter the Old Town and other historical areas of Prague; small art galleries where you could bargain over prices; factory crystal shops, etc.

Plastic bag envy was a common affliction here in the early days, and any bag that came into your possession was saved, cared for and carefully guarded. It was simply rare to get any bag of **any** material, to the point that you stared if you saw someone carrying a full shopping bag of particular quality and size along the street while you thought to yourself, "*I wonder where she got that bag?!*" while also wondering where you could get on like it. If you lost your bag or it became damaged, you might not manage to get a replacement until you had a reason to fly to Frankfurt or some other Western destination.

In that way, Prague was eco-friendly on the plastic bag front before everyone else and without knowing it … until a few years passed and plastic bags began to crop up – slowly at first – until they eventually began to be handed out every time you shopped! What luxury! Then the world and later Prague got serious about too many plastic bags in the environment, and various measures have been taken to curtail their use. They are still around – usually for a small fee – as are paper bags and net bags and store-branded reusable eco-friendly shopping bags. So in a short span of time (about 15 years), Prague has run the gamut on the plastic bag front that spanned decades in the West.

The rock bottom prices have gone, too, though you will find that Prague is still incredibly cheap for much of the shopping you'll do here, especially when it comes to locally-produced items. Crystal and glass, in particular, are a real bargain, especially considering the quality and the fact that most of it is mouth-blown, hand-cut and hand-polished.

These days the city center is packed with more crystal shops than you would think could survive, but they do thanks to the huge numbers of tourists who visit year-round. And more of them keep opening. And now you can find some really unique and wonderful shops offering a wide range of other types of goods, some local and some not, including a handful of establishments selling a quirky assortment of items from all over the world. And of course the city is littered with souvenirs, from junky to not bad.

If you like to collect treasures on your travels, valuable or not, local or not, you can find everything from antiques to a custom-made marionette of your favorite opera character or historical figure. The beautiful Pařížská (Paris) Street, always a street of wealth and style (except for the wealth part during communism), is where you'll find Hermes, Tiffany, Cartier, Patek Philippe and just about all of the other luxury brand names you know.

The shops I list here are my personal favorites, either because of some uniqueness, Czech or otherwise, that they and the goods they sell possess, or because they are the best shops carrying the things that the Czechs are known for (such as crystal, garnets and marionettes). I try to cover a range of items and interests, so that hopefully your particular interests will be included here. So, you'll find everything from antiques to Cuban cigars to model trains listed in this book. And if there is some category that you are interested in that I do not cover, please email me at krysti.brice@seznam.cz and let me know. I will consider adding it if Prague happens to have some worthy representatives in your category.

2 ABOUT THIS BOOK

Thank you for buying my book. I hope you will find it useful. Here are a few notes to help you make the most of this guide and your shopping in Prague:

As I say in my Prague guidebook, "Prague Travel Tips," **things change quickly in Prague,** and information is not always forthcoming (this is the land of Kafka, after all). Given the volume of tourist traffic and the nature of the local economy, which is still in a learning curve, businesses open and close quickly and often, only to be replaced by the next café or crystal shop. This is especially true of smaller shops, which tend to offer the most unique items, and which therefore are more likely to be highly represented herein. So, although **I will do my best to keep this book updated** after this initial March 2018 publication, I apologize in advance if any establishment listed here has disappeared by the time you visit. And if that is the case, I would love it if you would contact me to let me know so that I can make the change.

I have included addresses, phone numbers and websites, etc. (where available), for all of the shops included here. Shop hours are listed using the 24-hour clock. The telephone country code for the Czech Republic is 420. In the interest of efficiency, I did not include the country code at the beginning of each phone entry. So just know that if you try to call any number in the Czech Republic from *outside* the Czech Republic, you need to dial "420" at the beginning (preceded by whatever prefix you need depending on where you are calling from). Of course, within the Czech Republic, you do not need to dial "420" (or any other prefix, such as "011").

I have checked all tram stops listed here against the public transport website (and against my own knowledge and experience). However, the tram network went through a major reorganization in 2017, and I did notice that some of the shops' individual websites have not yet been updated to reflect the recent tram route changes and therefore still provide the former (now invalid) tram numbers for reaching their locations. So, in cases where you are using a particular listing's website for public transport connections, you might want to double check it against the public transport website (www.dpp.cz/en) or the information contained in this book.

And finally, major reorganizations notwithstanding, tram networks, it seems, need to be incessantly dug up and re-laid every three or four years on a rotating basis, and so it's almost inevitable that a particular tram will not be going where it is supposed to go at some time or another during the year. To make things worse, this usually happens in the warm summer months, when most visitors like you will be here for your summer holidays! And unfortunately (bohužel), nothing about the changes will be provided in English. Rather, information will be posted at tram stops in long paragraphs of unusually and unnecessarily complicated Czech that even the Czechs have difficulty deciphering (evidenced by the fact that large numbers of locals will be gathered around the posted information and staring at it for long periods of time with blank or quizzical looks on their faces). So, if you don't see your desired tram number listed at a stop where it should be, or if you get on a tram and it takes you somewhere other than where you were intending to go, my advice is to ask somebody for help.

Happy shopping!

3 SOME PRAGUE HISTORY

Though this is a book about shopping in Prague, you might nevertheless like to know a bit about the history of the place where you'll be doing your shopping, so I've included this chapter on Czech history. Note, however, that Czech history is extremely complex, as is Prague's. So for the purposes of this book, I'll try to keep it brief and relatively simple.

Prague, the capital of the Czech Republic and of the lands historically known as Bohemia (or the Czech lands), was founded when the Czech Slavic tribes were unified under the Přemyslid dynasty during the Romanesque period. The other regions that make up the current-day Czech Republic are Moravia and Silesia.

Over the centuries following its founding, Prague and the Czech lands have had mixed fortunes, at times being independent but most often being under the yoke of other lands. Although it has long been an important center in the heart of Europe, two periods in particular stand out as times during which Prague flourished and experienced great prosperity and importance. These were the 14th and the 16th centuries, under the reigns of Charles IV and Rudolf II, respectively. During these leaders' respective reigns, Prague was not only the capital of Bohemia but was also the seat of the Holy Roman Empire.

A History of Glass

The Czechs have been making glass dating back to at least the 13th century, but it was during the Renaissance, and Rudolf's reign in particular, that Bohemia "became famous for its beautiful and colorful glass."[1] And it was Rudolf's gem cutter, Caspar Lehmann, who "adapted to glass the technique of gem engraving," and "the Czech lands became the dominant producer of decorative glassware," earning an "international reputation in high Baroque style" in the 17th and 18th centuries.[1] As a result, you'll see many crystal and glass shops listed in this book.

Europe's First Reformation

Jan Hus was a Czech Protestant reformer who predated Martin Luther by a century (in fact, Luther was inspired by Hus). His reform movement sparked the Hussite Wars which erupted a decade or so after Hus was burned at the stake for heresy in 1415. Knowing he would otherwise burn, Hus was given a chance to recant all he had said about the excesses of the Catholic Church, yet he chose to stand for his beliefs and face the fire. For this reason, I believe that we all owe a debt to Jan Hus when it comes to the concepts of free speech, freedom of religion, etc.

From Hus's death until 1620, Bohemia was the site of many protestant uprisings. The so-called Second Defenestration of Prague in 1618, when two Catholic officials and their secretary were thrown out of a window at Prague Castle by Protestant rebels, is credited with starting the Thirty Years' War.

Baroque Drama

Early in that war, the Czech Protestant armies were soundly defeated by the Hapsburg Catholics at the Battle of White Mountain. Subsequently, Prague and the Czech lands fell under the firm grip of the Hapsburgs (until World War I), and the Counterreformation ensued. In Prague and the Czech lands, this meant (among other things) inundating the territory and the capital with Baroque architecture.

The Baroque style, with its beauty, drama and excess, was seen as the perfect propaganda tool in the Hapsburgs' attempt to re-Catholicize the Czech population. The Baroque was meant to impress, overwhelm and brag – and it does. But especially in the Czech lands, where the population was 90% protestant by the time the Thirty Years' War broke out, extra persuasion was needed.

Resistant to religion in general and to Catholicism in particular after so many centuries of religious strife and foreign (i.e., Catholic, in Czech minds) occupation, the Czechs were a hard sell when it came to all religion but especially when it came to Catholicism. For that reason, Baroque architecture dominates Prague and the entire Czech Republic (with rare exception, every Czech town and village has at least one richly decorated Baroque church in its center), and the Baroque of Bohemia is not only prevalent, it is also particularly intense compared to other places.

During the Counterreformation, much of Prague's Old Town was remodeled in the Baroque style. But while Old Town got a mere facelift, the Lesser Quarter (Malá Strana) was almost completely rebuilt in a Baroque building boom. Due to its proximity to Prague Castle, the Malá Strana was the neighborhood of choice for the noble families of the Czech and other Hapsburg lands who wished to reside close to the Castle (and therefore close to the seat of power). So after the Catholic armies' victories in the Thirty Years' War, land in the Malá Strana was given to noble families, victorious generals and various orders of the Catholic Church, each of whom proceeded to build grand palaces, beautiful gardens, impressive churches and monasteries on it.

Interestingly (and luckily, in my view), there has been almost no new construction in the Malá Strana since the 18th century, so it remains one of the most beautiful Baroque preserves in all of Europe. Partly for this reason, many of the movies and television shows that are filmed in Prague (and there are a LOT of them – more than you realize) are filmed in the Malá Strana. Almost all of Milos Forman's Oscar-winning film "Amadeus" was shot in Prague, much of it in Malá Strana.

A History of Music

And if Czechs were going to be "persuaded" to be Catholic, they were going to need to be able to understand "Catholic" music (i.e., Baroque music at the time), reasoned the powers that were. So the Hapsburgs instituted a program of music instruction for all Czech schoolchildren. The result was a land of very musically-literate and musically-talented people, and this is one reason you will notice that classical music concerts, most of them of quite high quality, are ubiquitous in Prague.

And as a side note, and not surprisingly, shops selling musical instruments and violin workshops were quite prevalent in Prague when I first arrived in the early 1990s. Sadly, the number of these quaint Old World shops is dwindling, but a few of those still holding on are listed in this book.

Occupations and Freedom

From the 16th to the 20th centuries, Prague and the Czech lands were part of the Austro-Hungarian Empire. When that empire dissolved after World War I, the country of Czechoslovakia was founded, with Prague as its capital. World War II brought Nazi occupation and the decimation of the country's Jewish population, followed by forty years of Communist rule that eventually included occupation by Soviet troops beginning in 1968. In 1989, the fall of the Berlin Wall brought freedom, followed shortly thereafter by the breakup of Czechoslovakia and the formation of the Czech Republic in 1993. (The Soviet troops took their time leaving – the last of the soldiers departed in 1991, some 23 years after they rolled onto Wenceslas Square, and two years after the fall of the Communist regime.)

Since then, Prague has evolved rapidly into the quite cosmopolitan capital that it is today – or perhaps it returned to its pre-communist cosmopolitan nature, for it still retains some of its Old World charm. That's due partly to its culture, as Václav Havel, the former-dissident-turned-president once alluded to when he proclaimed, "Prague is a village." And it's also due to the fact that, historically, Prague was made up of five smaller, formerly independent (not totally independent, but rather like the boroughs of New York City) towns that are now unified: Prague Castle (Hradčany), Old Town (Staré Město), the Jewish Quarter (Josefov), the Lesser Quarter or Little Town (Malá Strana) and New Town (Nové Město).

Because each of these towns had its own city administration, mayor, town hall, guilds and purpose, each of them developed separately and therefore differently from each other, which is still evident even today in each area's architecture and atmosphere. And Prague never suffered significant damage in any 20th-century war, which means it escaped the especially destructive capability of the weaponry available in World War II.

All of these factors combined meant that an opportunity to impose a "unified vision" of a grand, "modern" city onto Prague never really presented itself. As a result (and thankfully, I suppose), even the current layout of the streets in the historic center is the result of medieval town planning, which you'll sense as you walk around the unique city that exists today.

Notes:
1.   Wikipedia, The Free Encyclopedia, s.v. "Bohemian Glass," (accessed February 4, 2018), https://en.wikipedia.org/wiki/Bohemian_glass

4 CRYSTAL, FINE GLASS AND PORCELAIN

As was mentioned in the chapter on Prague history, the Czech Republic is famous for its crystal and glass. It was in the Baroque period that Czech glassware became as prestigious as jewelry, and Czech crystal chandeliers could be found in the palaces of King Louis XV, Empress Maria Theresa of Austria, and Elizabeth of Russia.[1] There are crystal shops everywhere.

The quality is, for the most part, very high. And even though prices have gone up in recent years, beautiful Czech crystal is still a bargain by comparison, especially considering that almost all of it is hand-blown, hand-cut and hand-polished. In addition to beautiful wine glasses, vases and chandeliers, you can also pick up stunning crystal jewelry.

The most famous brands of Czech crystal are Bohemia Crystal, Moser and Preciosa. And most shops will ship it for you if you end up buying too much to carry with you – for a fee, of course, but you will save the VAT (value-added tax), which can be up to 15%.

Czech porcelain is also quite good. The best brands are Thun, made near the western Bohemian spa town of Karlovy Vary (Carlsbad); and Český Porcelán Dubí, which produces the Czech

Republic's unique blue onion pattern of hand-painted everyday tableware. Here is a list of Prague's best shops:

Erpet

When it comes to buying Czech crystal in Prague, Erpet is THE place. Located on Old Town Square, Erpet has a huge variety and selection of crystal and porcelain (for which the Czechs are also rather famous). Whether you like traditional or modern, cut or polished, colored or clear, Erpet has it – from the more formal (and pricier) styles to the simple, uncut everyday wine and water glasses. And Erpet carries virtually every Czech brand, from the famous highly-cut Bohemia Crystal to the pricier Aida brand, famous for its etched pieces. Even if you end up buying so much that you need to pay to have it shipped home, you will still probably pay a lot less than you would if you bought comparable pieces in the US or elsewhere outside of the Czech Republic.

Traditional Czech cut crystal – reprinted with permission of Pixabay CC. www.pixabay.com

And if you don't ship, don't forget that you can get your VAT back at the airport if you buy more than CZK 2,000 worth of goods (at almost any shop, crystal or otherwise – see "Tax-Free

Shopping"). But shipping offers the added advantage not having to bother with filling out forms and getting stamps at the airport – if you ship, the tax will be deducted automatically at the time of purchase, eliminating the hassle of collecting the tax yourself.

As a general rule, the price on the goods you see in any shop or restaurant, whether you're ordering a beer or buying a chandelier, already includes the VAT in the price marked on the goods or listed on the menu. The tax will not be added when you pay as is done in the U.S. What you see is what you pay. Also, your restaurant bill will show a breakdown of the total (gross) amount of the bill indicating the net amount and the amount that is tax. But it is just a breakdown – the tax is already included in the total, which is the amount you pay. Many visitors mistake the tax in the breakdown for the tip, which is **not** included in your bill (though a very few unsavory restaurants will add a small cover charge to your bill, but this is uncommon – and worth a complaint, in my view, which I usually lodge).

Erpet also has beautiful **crystal chandeliers** (which you will find are everywhere in Prague, by the way – not just in the venues where you'd expect to find them, such as fancy theaters and concert halls, but also in small restaurants and shops), and these beauties, with their handmade pieces of crystal, are a bargain compared to what they would cost you at home, even with the shipping cost (the prices in Prague are a fraction of what you'd pay in your home country, so if you've got a dining room you're redecorating, it's worth considering shipping a Bohemian crystal chandelier home!).

If you're looking for something for a smaller budget, consider a single beautifully-cut vase or a set of shot glasses. Jewelry made of **Czech crystal beads** will only set you back $10-$20. And speaking of jewelry, Erpet also carries **Czech garnets** ("granát"). While some garnet settings can be pricey, they, like the crystal, are also quite affordable by comparison, so a garnet item does not have to destroy your budget. And some of the smaller settings are very reasonable indeed. See "Garnets and Other Jewelry, Clothing and Shoes." Finally, a good selection of Czech porcelain is also available in Erpet in a large room off the back end of the store, so be sure not to miss it.

If you think you might be interested in Czech crystal, or anything at Erpet, email me at krysti.brice@seznam.cz, and I can send you some discount coupons, so you can save even more! And when you visit the store, be aware that it is HUGE, so don't let it overwhelm you. Try to home in on what you want and go straight to that section. And be aware that sometimes Erpet is packed with large tour groups. So if it's full when you visit and you don't like crowds, consider returning in an hour or so, and the big crowd will have probably moved on.

Erpet Bohemia Crystal
Old Town Square 27
Hours: daily 10:00 – 23:00
Phone: 224 229 755, 224 229 755
Tram: 2, 17 or 18 to Staroměstská
Metro: Green ("A") line to Staroměstská, or green ("A") and yellow ("B") line to Můstek
Email: info@erpetcrystal.cz
www.erpetcrystal.cz

Moser

Produced in the spa town of Karlovy Vary (Carlsbad), Moser is considered by some to be the finest crystal in the world, on a par with or better than Waterford. And it is quite pricey, even by the relatively cheaper crystal prices in the Czech Republic. It is much more expensive than Bohemia Crystal and other Czech brands. And you can see and feel the difference – Moser is more than "a cut above." **But you'll still pick it up cheaper here than you will outside of the Czech Republic,** especially when you throw in the VAT savings.

For a unique experience, even if Moser is out of your budget, you might want to visit the original Moser store on Na Příkopě which, in addition to the crystal, exhibits a bit of Old World luxury and charm that survived even the communist times (and has now been substantially refurbished). Moser also has a newer store on

Old Town Square.

Moser

Na Příkopě 12
Phone: 224 211 293
Hours: Mon.-Fri. 10:00 – 20:00, Sat.-Sun.10:00 – 19:00
Metro: Green ("A") line or Yellow ("B") line to Můstek
Email: pha-prikopy@moser-glass.com
www.moser-glass.com

Staroměstské Náměstí 15 (Old Town Square 15)
Hours: Mon.-Fri. 10:00 – 20:00, Sat.-Sun.10:00 – 19:00
Phone: 221 890 891
Tram: 2, 17 or 18 to Staroměstská
Metro: Green ("A") line to Staroměstská
Email: pha-star@moser-glass.com
www.moser-glass.com

Preciosa

This brand of crystal is carried at Erpet and many other crystal shops in Prague, but you might want to visit their newest showroom in Old Town to take in its amazing light fixtures, especially the GINORMOUS chandelier that you cannot miss when you walk in the door.

Preciosa

Rytířská 29
Hours: Not listed
Phone: 488 118 106
Metro: Green ("A") line or Yellow ("B") line to Můstek
Email: prodejna.praha@preciosa.com
www.preciosa.com

ART GLASS

The Czechs also produce an endless array of high-quality glass, most of it hand-blown.   It is, of course, cheaper than the crystal,

17

but the quality of Czech glass is also evident. Most crystal shops carry a range of fine glass in addition to crystal. A few makers of unique pieces of "art" glass and "designer" crystal have their own shops showcasing their work. Some of the best places to look are:

Artěl

Try not to miss this very unique design shop featuring current versions of classic Czech design items (both crystal and fine glass). An American artist from New York opened Artěl in 1998, and she has done some amazing things with her collection. Artěl's products are very unique, combining the exquisite quality of mouth-blown, hand-decorated crystal with sophisticated, modern design. There are two locations, one in Malá Strana just below the Charles Bridge and one on Platnéřská Street in Old Town.

Artěl Concept Store
Platnéřská 7, Prague 1
Hours: daily 10:00 – 19:00
Phone: 226 254 700
Tram: 2, 17 or 18 to Staroměstská
Metro: Green ("A") line to Staroměstská
Bus: 207 to Staroměstská
Email: info@artelglass.com
www.artelglass.com

Artěl Malá Strana
U Lužického Semináře 7, Prague 1
Hours: daily 10:00 – 19:00
Phone: 251 554 008
Tram: 12, 15, 20, 22 or 23 to Malostranské Náměstí

Bořek Šípek Showroom & Gallery

Though the famous designer and architect who created these fabulously unique works of glass died in 2016, his designs are still being reproduced by Šípek glassworks. You simply have to see Šípek's work to know what it's like. In addition to their e-shop, you can find the real thing at one remaining shop in Prague on Valentinská Street in Old Town.

Bořek Šípek Showroom & Gallery
Valentinská 11
Hours: Mon.-Fri. 10:00 – 18:00, Sat.-Sun. 11:00 – 17:00
Phone: 224 814 099
Tram: 2, 17 or 18 to Staroměstská
Metro: Green ("A") line to Staroměstská
Bus: 207 to Staroměstská
E-mail: info@stvol.eu
www.stvol.eu
www.sipekglass.cz (e-shop)

Material

This is one of the best art glass makers, located in Týnský Dvůr (sometimes also called Ungelt, especially on maps), just behind the Týn Church on Old Town Square. These unique pieces are very special, as is the shop itself. Material also has a great selection of glass beads.

Material
Týn 1
Hours: daily 10:00 – 20:00
Phone: 608 664 766
Tram: 6, 8, 15 or 26 to Náměstí Republiky
Metro: Yellow ("B") line to Náměstí Republiky
Bus: 194 to Masná
www.i-material.com

PORCELAIN

As was mentioned above, Erpet also carries porcelain. And here's another place you might want to check out:

19

Material interior

Dům Porcelánu

The name means "House of Porcelain," and it really fits: Dům Porcelánu's selection is almost exclusively porcelain, and it has the largest assortment of porcelain in any one place in Prague. Their main product is the original blue onion pattern from Český Porcelán (see Erpet above), but they have other brands and styles as well. A visit to this shop means a visit to Vinohrady, one of Prague's many neighborhoods outside the historic center.

Dům Porcelánu
Jugoslávská 16
Hours: Mon.-Fri. 9:00 – 19:00, Sat. 9:00 – 17:00, Sun. 14:00 – 17:00
Phone: 221 505 320
Tram: 4, 6, 10, 16, 22 and 23 to I.P. Pavlova
Metro: Red ("C") line to I.P. Pavlova or Green ("A") line to Náměstí Míru
www.dumporcelanu.cz

Czech blue onion porcelain

Notes:
1. Wikipedia, The Free Encyclopedia, s.v. "Bohemian Glass," (accessed February 4, 2018), https://en.wikipedia.org/wiki/Bohemian_glass

5 GARNETS AND OTHER JEWELRY, CLOTHING AND SHOES

When it comes to jewelry, the Czech Republic is known for garnets. Most Czech garnets, which tend to be a dark red, are mined in the town of Turnov, whose surrounding mountains have yielded the stones for centuries. Some garnets from other mines elsewhere in the Czech Republic are so dark that they are almost black in color. Most settings are on the more traditional side, but you can find modern settings and designs, too. Typically garnets are set in gold, silver or gold-plated silver.

An interesting historical note is that the presence of the semi-precious stones in Turnov brought Jewish settlers to the town to participate in the jewelry trade. Today the town has a renovated Jewish Quarter and the remnants of a Jewish cemetery over which, unfortunately, the communists erected a highway. Sadly, Turnov was one of the first towns in Nazi-occupied former Czechoslovakia whose Jewish inhabitants were deported during the Holocaust, and almost the entirety of the town's Jewish population was wiped out in very short order. So if you are interested in Jewish history and culture, a visit to Turnov's Jewish Quarter is worth the trip.

Erpet

As mentioned in the chapter on crystal, this shop
Square also carries Czech garnets. The garnets in
store are mined in Turnov, whereas the room off the back of .
store that also contains Czech porcelain has garnets mined both in
Turnov and in another mine that yields even darker stones.

Between the two in the center of the store you'll also find
amber. Erpet has some beautiful amber pieces, but keep in mind
that, generally, most amber for sale in Prague is not usually from
the Czech Republic. Most likely it is from Poland. Moldevite is a
beautiful green stone that is mined locally, and Erpet has jewelry
set with this stone, sometimes accompanied by diamonds, in the
front of the store.

Erpet interior – photo reprinted with the permission of Erpet
Group a.s.

As you walk around Prague, you'll notice that garnet shops are
almost as ubiquitous as crystal shops. Years ago there were only a
few shops specializing in garnet jewelry, and those original shops
were all quite reliable. But included in the new explosion of garnet
shops are many rip-off places selling fakes. My advice is to stay
away from them and shop for garnets at Erpet or the other shop

listed below. Erpet provides a certificate of authentication with all of the garnet jewelry it sells.

Erpet Bohemia Crystal
Old Town Square 27
Hours: daily 10:00 – 23:00
Phone: 224 229 755, 224 229 755
Tram: 2, 17 or 18 to Staroměstská
Metro: Green ("A") line to Staroměstská, or green ("A") and yellow ("B") line to Můstek
Email: info@erpetcrystal.cz
www.erpetcrystal.cz

The other good shop for garnets is Turnov Granát:

Turnov Granát
Dlouhá 28
Hours: Mon.-Sat. 9:00 – 19:00, Sun. 10:00 – 17:00
Phone: 222 315 612
Tram: 6, 8, 15, or 26 to Dlouhá Třída
Bus: 207 to Dlouhá Třída

AleAle

It's hard to describe with words just how beautiful and special the glass bead jewelry pieces made by this local artist are. And each piece by Alena Chládková is unique – the artist never copies the exact same design or motif – so whatever you take home will be one of a kind. And the prices are incredibly reasonable considering the amount of work that goes into each piece. Alena's work is so good that it was featured in British *Vogue* a few years back. She has two shops in Prague (both in the Malá Strana) showcasing her necklaces, bracelets, earrings and more. The main location is listed here:

AleAle
Lázeňská 2
Hours: Mon.-Sat. 10:30-18:30, closed Sunday

Phone: Not listed
Tram: 12, 15, 20, 22 or 23 to Hellichova
Email: aleale@aleale.cz
www.aleale.cz

Baťa

Baťa is a world-famous Czech brand of shoes originally manufactured in the Czech Republic – well, famous just about everywhere in the world except the US (I'm not sure why, but I'm sure there's an interesting story behind that fact). Founded in the town of Zlín in the Moravian region of the Czech Republic by Tomáš Baťa in 1894, the company now boasts more than 5,000 retail stores. Tomáš Baťa himself is legendary for being a visionary business leader (he is sometimes called "the Henry Ford of Europe"), and the remnants of his workers' village in Zlín have now become trendy, highly-sought-after retro housing.

Baťa shoes are both stylish and affordable, and like Baťa's workers' village, the company's flagship store in Prague on Wenceslas Square (Václavské Náměstí) is also noteworthy for its ahead-of-its-time 1920's Functionalist design.

Baťa
Václavské Náměstí 6
Hours: Mon.-Sat. 9:00 – 21:00; Sun. 10:00 – 21:00
Phone: 221 088 478
Tram: 3, 5, 6, 9, 14, 24 to Václavské Náměstí
Metro: Green ("A") line or Yellow ("B") line to Můstek
www.bata.cz

Jaroslava – Design by Jaroslava Procházková

Jaroslava Procházková is one of the most popular and successful Czech fashion designers, and her signature women's knitwear is marked by timeless style, unique and sophisticated color combinations and quality workmanship, (custom tailoring is part of her shop's service). Jaroslava is located in the Lucerna Pasáž,

25

ıch is itself worth a visit to see its stunning original Art Nouveau interior, as well as a famous (equestrian, of sorts) work by the Czech contemporary artist, David Černý.

Jaroslava – Design by Jaroslava Procházková
Vodičkova 36
Hours: Not listed
Phone: 731 483 847
Tram: 3, 5, 6, 9, 14, 24 to Václavské Náměstí
Metro: Green ("A") line or Yellow ("B") line to Můstek (exit to Vodičkova Street)
www.jaroslava.cz/en

Otherwise, when it comes to **Czech fashion and Czech designers**, it would be worth your while wandering around the area of Old Town **bordered by Dlouhá, Dušní, Vězenská and Rámová Streets.** It's also a nice area of town to wander around, as it's not completely inundated with tourists and tourist shops – yet.

6 MARIONETTES, HANDICRAFTS AND TOYS

In addition to crystal and garnets, marionettes are the other top item that one would want to bring back as a memento from the Czech Republic, as these are another of the top items the country is known for. And the Czechs have always been good at handicrafts, such as beautifully decorated (by hand) Easter eggs and wooden toys.

PUPPETS (MARIONETTES)

Czechs love puppets and their puppet theaters (actually, marionettes are the more prevalent type of puppet found here, but I'll use the words interchangeably). Many festivals and other events will include puppet shows for children, and there's even a theater in town that regularly puts on the opera "Don Giovanni" with puppets! Consequently, puppets are popular Prague souvenirs.

Most souvenir shops and outdoor markets sell puppets of varying quality and size, both wooden and plastic (which tend to be cheaper). A few shops specialize in the more authentic wooden, hand-carved ones. But in the center of town these are dwindling, as they can't support the high rents that have come along with the tourist trade.

Czech marionettes – reprinted with permission of Pixabay CC

But a few good shops with handmade wooden puppets still exist: a couple in Malá Strana – one just under the Charles Bridge on U Lužického Semináře (on your right as you come off the bridge on the Malá Strana side of the river) and one on Nerudova Street – and a few in Old Town.

Truhlář Marionety
U Lužického Semináře 5
Hours: daily 10:00 – 21:00
Tram: 12, 15, 20, 22 or 23 to Malostranské Náměstí
Metro: Green ("A") line to Malostranská
www.marionety.com

AMI Loutky - Obchod Loutkami
Nerudova 47
Hours: daily: 10:00 – 18:00
Phone: 775 552 471
Tram: 12, 15, 20, 22 or 23 to Malostranské Náměstí

Czech Marionettes
Karoliny Světlé 14
Hours: Mon.-Fri. 10:00 – 18:00, Sat. 11:00 – 17:00, closed Sunday
Phone: 604 230 945
Tram: 2, 9, 17, 18, 22 or 23 to Národní Třída or 2, 17 or 18 to Karlovy Lázně

National Marionette Theater

If you are a puppet person, you will want to check out the National Marionette Theater, which, without a doubt, has the best puppet show in town. It is certainly the most popular one, and sadly, there aren't too many others around these days in any case. This theater puts on Don Giovanni most nights (I have seen it and really enjoyed it), and they also occasionally put on a performance of the Magic Flute.

In addition to performances, the National Marionette Theater offers a "Marionette Tour Prague" and a puppet workshop, both of which are worth checking out.

National Marionette Theater
Žatecká 1
Phone: 224 819 322
Mobile: 724 367 126
Tram: 2, 17 or 18 to Staroměstská
Metro: Green ("A") line to Staroměstská
Email: festival@mozart.cz
www.mozart.cz

HANDICRAFTS

There are many handicrafts that the Czechs (and some surrounding countries) are known for, such as decorated Easter eggs, wooden toys and ceramics.

Manufaktura interior

Manufaktura

Manufaktura sells cosmetics and beauty products that are modeled on the same theme as Botanicus (see below and "Health and Beauty") and also features many traditional Czech handicrafts, such as wonderful Czech wooden toys and the beautifully hand-decorated Easter eggs (most of them made from real eggshells). In fact, everything in this chain's shops must be of Czech origin and produced by their specially selected suppliers *"comprising small craftsmen, former masters of folk craft, small Czech companies and other bearers of tradition,"* as per their website.

Manufaktura has many locations throughout Old Town and Malá Strana (on Mostecká Street leading to the Charles Bridge). Their products make good gifts to take back home, including beer shampoo. The most central locations are listed here:

Manufaktura
Melantrichova 17
Hours: daily 10:00 – 20:00
Phone: 230 234 376
Metro: Green ("A") line or Yellow ("B") line to Můstek
www.manufaktura.cz

Karlova 26
Hours: daily 10:00 – 20:00
Phone: 601 310 605
Tram: 2, 17 or 18 to Karlovy Lázně or 2, 17 or 18 to Staroměstská
Metro: Green ("A") line to Staroměstská

Mostecká 17
Hours: daily 10:00 – 20:00
Phone: 601 310 609
Tram: 12, 15, 20, 22 or 23 to Malostranské Náměstí

Botanicus

Handmade paper and soap, essential oils and candles made of beeswax are just a few of the items you'll find in this shop. The

31

main store is located in Týnský Dvůr (also known as Ungelt) just off of Old Town Square. See more under "Health and Beauty."

Botanicus Prague - Ungelt

Týn 3 (in Týnský Dvůr, also called Ungelt, especially on maps)
Hours: daily 10:00 – 20:00
Phone: 234 767 446
Tram: 6, 8, 15, 26 to Náměstí Republiky
Metro: Yellow ("B") line to Náměstí Republiky
Email: praha.ungelt@botanicus.cz
www.botanicus.cz/en

Fajans Majolica (Ceramic Workshop of Juraj Vanya)

In addition to finely cut and etched crystal and hand-carved wooden marionettes, the Czechs (and Slovaks, with whom they used to share a nation, the former Czechoslovakia), are also quite talented when it comes to traditional hand-painted ceramics. Without a doubt, the workshop of Juraj Vanya has some of the most beautiful and intricately hand-decorated items in town.

And they're also practical – you might actually use a coffee mug you bought here regularly, as opposed to some crystal champagne flutes that you bring out only on special occasions – and in my opinion the prices are extremely low for the amount and quality of work that goes into each piece. Vanya works in traditional folk-art patterns, so these items also make great traditional gifts to take home. And in addition to large plates and platters, there are also small items, like salt and pepper shakers, that are easy to pack.

Fajans Majolica

Týn 4 (in Týnský Dvůr, also called Ungelt)
Hours: daily 10.00 – 19.00
Phone: 224 815 728
Tram: 6, 8, 15, 26 to Náměstí Republiky
Yellow ("B") line to Náměstí Republiky
www.fajans.cz

TOYS

Czech toys are simply marvelous, and several different shops will carry a range of them, from the neat hand-carved wooden ones to the retro 1950s communist-era metal cars and tram sets. Here are a few shops to check out:

Czech Zetor toy tractors at Hračky – Houpací Kůň

Hračky – Houpací Kůň (The Rocking Horse Toy Shop)

This is one of the best toy shops in Prague. It's locally-owned and features only Czech and (a few) German-made toys. The owner carefully selects every product that he sells. It features toy models of the famous Czech-made Škoka car, puppets, hand-made kaleidoscopes, classic Czech toy tractors and trams and much more. The toy tractors are one of my favorite Czech toys – they have five gears, including reverse! Hračky – Houpací Kůň is located in Hradčany, the castle district of Prague, so you can stop by there when you visit Prague Castle.

Hračky – Houpací Kůň (The Rocking Horse Toy Shop)
Loretánské Náměstí 3
Hours: daily 10:00 – 18:00
Phone: 603 515 745
Tram: 22 or 23 to Pohořelec

Hračky u Zlatého Lva (Toys at the Golden Lion)

This is a rather large toy shop on Celetná Street, the main drag between the Powder Tower and Old Town Square. It has a large array of uniquely Czech toys, including marionettes (mostly of the cheaper plastic variety) and puppet sets. Most of the toys are very affordable and very packable.

Hračky u Zlatého Lva
Celetná 32
Hours: daily 9:00 – 20:00
Phone: 224 239 469
Tram: 6, 8, 15 or 26 to Náměstí Republiky
Yellow ("B") line to Náměstí Republiky

Manufaktura

As mentioned above, Manufaktura sells wonderful Czech wooden toys that are almost all handmade. The location on Karlova Street has the largest selection of toys (on the upper level).

Karlova 26
Hours: daily 10:00 – 20:00
Phone: 601 310 605
Tram: 2, 17 or 18 to Karlovy Lázně or Staroměstská
Metro: Green ("A") line to Staroměstská
www.manufaktura.cz

V Ungeltu

This is actually a dual shop that has wooden toys on one side and marionettes on the other. Both offer a good, quality selection.

V Ungeltu

Týn 10 (in Týnský Dvůr, also called Ungelt)

Hours: daily 10:00 – 20:00

Tram: 6, 8, 15 or 26 to Náměstí Republiky

Yellow ("B") line to Náměstí Republiky

7 SOUVENIRS

Technically speaking, just about everything in this book could be considered a souvenir. But in terms of the types of items that meet a stricter definition of that word and that are not unique to the Czech Republic – other than the words "Prague" or "Czech Republic" or perhaps a picture of the Charles Bridge or another famous Prague landmark or national treasure (like beer!) on them – Prague has plenty of these, too. So, you can buy tee-shirts and fridge magnets literally EVERYWHERE in the historic center of Prague.

And then there are the items that have nothing to do with Prague but which sellers can get away with plying as "authentic" Czech souvenirs due to the huge numbers of tourists who visit each year. These include the ubiquitous "nesting dolls" that are actually Russian (and on the pricier side amber, which is mostly from Poland). By all means, if you want a nesting doll, please go ahead and get one. But just be aware that they have nothing whatsoever to do the Czech Republic, except for the fact that the Russians once occupied the country for more than two decades. Some of the more non-traditional dolls are those painted with the images of famous figures, such as Mikhail Gorbachev or former Czech president Vaclav Havel, or with players from your favorite sports teams back home.

Because most items other than ordinary souvenirs are covered elsewhere in this book, and because there are literally hundreds of everyday souvenir shops in Prague rendering them too many to name, this chapter is very short. But one notable shop is listed, as well as the areas/streets with the highest concentration of the more ubiquitous sellers.

Blue

This is a chain of nicer souvenir shops that has everything from good picture books of Prague to better quality T-shirts and postcards, and, yes, art glass. Blue has locations all over Old Town (Celetná Street, Malé Náměstí and Melantrichova Street) and on Mostecká Street in Malá Strana (on the right as you walk off of the Charles Bridge) to name a few. The Malé Náměstí location is listed here, along with their website where you can find more Blue stores.

Blue
Malé Náměstí 14
Hours: vary by location
Phone: 224 224 580
Tram: 2, 17 or 18 to Staroměstská
Metro: Green ("A") line to Staroměstská
Bus: 207 to Staroměstská
www.bluepraha.cz

SOUVENIR STREETS

If you want just a small, inexpensive, funny or even junky souvenir to take home, the greatest concentrations of sellers of such items can be found in the following locations:

- **Celetná, Melantrichova and Karlova Streets in Old Town,**
- **Mostecká and Nerudova Streets in Malá Strana (the Lesser Quarter),**
- **Havel's Market in Old Town.**

The streets above are all lined with souvenir shops almost from end to end, mostly of the junky kind, but you just might find the tee-shirt or beer stein you're looking for. Mostecká and Karlova Streets are those extending off of the Malá Strana and Old Town sides of the Charles Bridge, respectively, so naturally souvenir sellers fill these streets.

The Blue shop on Melantrichova

Interestingly, on the **Charles Bridge (Karlův Most)** itself, the junkier kinds of souvenirs are absent (thankfully). This is because a special law applies to the bridge. All the items for sale on it must be: 1) created in the Czech Republic by someone who lives in the Czech Republic, and 2) sold by someone who lives in the Czech Republic. So trinkets made in China don't pass the test, and this quirk makes the Charles Bridge a good place to buy a painting or a photograph or to have a caricature of yourself done by a local artist.

As soon as you get off of the bridge, though, everything changes, and you will be barraged with all kinds of "stuff." On the Old Town side of the Charles Bridge you'll find a **passageway** that runs along the river that is one of the junkiest places on earth. But junky or not, I think you can find any souvenir you want there (if you can stand it).

Souvenirs for sale at Havel's Market

Havel's Market

Havel's Market is a lively place that has souvenirs such as beer steins and fridge magnets as well as artwork and fruits and vegetables. This outdoor market has been around since the 13th century, making it a historical site as well. See more in "Gourmet Food Shops and Grocery Stores.

8 ART, ANTIQUES AND COLLECTIBLES

Given its long history, its location in the middle of "Mitteleuropa," the craftsmanship of its people and its one-time wealth (before World War II, former Czechoslovakia was one of the wealthiest countries in the world), it follows that Prague is not short of valuable items for collectors of all kinds of finery.

ANTIQUES

As is probably evident by now, many of the more unique, individual types of shops that were quite plentiful here when I arrived are quickly falling by the wayside. To the extent that these unique shops do still exist, they are mostly outside of the historical (tourist) center of town, and antique shops fall into this gone-by-the-wayside category, unfortunately.

Even by the time I arrived in early 1992, most of the best antiques in the Czech Republic had already been bought up by German bargain seekers crossing the border to buy from locals who were eager to (legally) get their hands on hard Western currency. And many of us have "shoulda, woulda, coulda" stories about whole sets of Meissen porcelain or sterling silver tableware that we could have gotten for a song.

Those days are probably over, but there are still lots of beautiful and/or unique items around. Most of the antiques are rather pricey, but there are some junk (or treasure, depending on your perspective) and pawn shops in town, too.

Antik v Dlouhé (Antiques on Dlouhá)

This large antique shop is one that is friendlier on the budget compared to a lot of the others in Old Town. It's great for those who like to treasure hunt.

Antik v Dlouhé
Dlouhá 37
Hours: Mon.-Fri. 10:00 – 19:00, Sat.-Sun. 12:00 – 18:00
Phone: 774 431 776
Tram: 6, 8, 15, or 26 to Dlouhá Třída
Bus: 207 to Dlouhá Třída

Bric a Brac

Bric a Brac is called an antique shop but could just as easily be called a junk shop, but the good kind. This place is literally crammed with stuff, wall-to-wall and floor-to-ceiling, and true treasure hunters and shoppers who love the thrill of searching through the forest to find a (special) tree will definitely find something to take home from this Bric a Brac.

Bric a Brac
Týnská 7 (behind the Týn Church)
Hours: daily 11:00 – 18:00
Phone: 222 326 484
Tram: 6, 8, 15, 26 to Náměstí Republiky
Metro: Yellow ("B") line to Náměstí Republiky
Bus: 194 to Masná

Bric a Brac entrance

Kaprova and Meiselova Streets

Several antiques shops can be found on both of these streets (one within the Jewish Quarter and one bordering it). Wander down them to see if any particular shop catches your fancy.

By the way, the KFC on Kaprova Street is a great place to pop in and use the restroom if you need to (for free, at least as of this writing), and across the street from it is Ebel Coffee, which has some of the best coffee in Prague.

Vetešnictví

The name means "junk shop" and that's exactly what this place is. And it's fantastic. It has been here since I moved here and has stood the test of time. But as gentrification creeps in around it (on the edge of Malá Strana), I wonder how much longer it will last. But hopefully it will continue to hang on until you get here. Vetešnictví is crammed with junk of all kinds, but I've gotten a few finds here.

Vetešnictví Újezd
Vítězná 16
Phone: 257 310 611
Hours: Mon.-Fri. 10:00 – 17:00, closed Saturday and Sunday
Tram: 9, 12, 15, 20, 22 or 23 to Újezd

Zastavárna on Korunní

This no-name pawn shop (a "zastavárna" is basically the Czech version of a pawn shop) is a great place to rummage through all kinds of items that locals have hocked for a few crowns. This one literally has no name that I can find, but it has been around since at least the late 90s, and is one of a handful that has survived in the Vinohrady neighborhood, which used to be full of them. It has no address on the building, either, but you can't miss it (and the big sign that says "Zastavárna" at the corner of Korunní and Blanická, just a block east of Náměstí Míru.

Zastavárna on Korunní
Tram: 4, 10, 16 and 22 to Náměstí Míru
Metro: Green ("A) line to Náměstí Míru

After visiting the Zastavárna, you can continue up Korunní with Náměstí Míru at your back and check out a few more antique shops in the next two to three blocks on the right as you walk uphill, as well as a local art supply store ("výtvarné potřeby"). There are also a couple of interesting cafes, including a Vietnamese one serving delicious authentic Vietnamese coffee.

ART GALLERIES AND AUCTIONEERS

Like so much of Prague's culture, the art scene here is undergoing a transformation. While great strides have been made in this area since the Berlin Wall fell, the city still lacks a definable area where art galleries are concentrated. But Michalská Street in Old Town comes close. And generally art is more affordable here than in many other cities. Some of my favorite places to check out are listed below.

Dorotheum

The Prague subsidiary of Dorotheum, the largest auction house in Central Europe, was founded in 1992. If you're an antique lover, Dorotheum is expensive but won't disappoint.

Dorotheum
Ovocný Trh 2
Hours: Mon.-Fri. 10.00 – 19:00, Sat. 10:00 – 17:00, closed Sunday
Phone: 224 222 001
Metro: Green ("A") line or Yellow ("B") line to Můstek
www.dorotheum.com/cz

Galerie Jakubska – New Impressionism

Alexandr Onishenko's work is truly a "new impressionism," and personally I love it. But love it or not, his is truly a success story of hard work and perseverance, as well as a "shoulda, woulda, coulda" story for many of us expats who were living here when he arrived from Ukraine and started painting on the Charles Bridge.

Twenty years later, Onishenko has had exhibitions in London and other international capitals, and his work is widely collected in the US, Asia and other parts of Europe. What a few hundred dollars could have bought way-back-when now goes for thousands.

Dorotheum

Galerie Jakubska

Jakubská 4
Hours: daily 10:00 – 18:00
Phone: 224 827 926
Tram: 6, 8, 15, 26 to Náměstí Republiky
Metro: Yellow ("B") line to Náměstí Republiky
www.galeriejakubska.com

Galerie Jakubska

Galerie Art Praha

This gallery on Old Town Square has been here a while. It features the work of many collected Czech artists from the 19th century to the present day and is one of my favorites. You can't miss it at the corner of Old Town Square and Železná Street (and not far from the famous Astronomical Clock).

Galerie Art Praha

Staroměstské Náměstí 20
Hours: Mon.-Sat. 10:30 – 18:30, closed Sunday

Phone: 224 211 087
Metro: Green ("A") line to Staroměstská
Email: galerie@g-a-p.cz
www.galerie-art-praha.cz

AD Galerie on Uhelný Trh

This gallery, like Galerie Art Praha on Old Town Square, has also been around since the early days and has stood the test of time. It offers an array of contemporary painting, ceramics and other art forms from only **Czech artists**, a point of pride for them. This distinction is probably deemed necessary due to the fact that most of the art you'll find in small galleries in much of the tourist area is by artists from the former Soviet Union (mainly from Ukraine, Armenia and Russia) who moved to Prague in the early 90s. There is nothing wrong in those artists selling their work, of course, and I find most of them to be quite talented, but if you're looking for "Czech" art by Czech artists, you'll want to be aware of the origin of the creator of the work.

AD Galerie
Uhelný Trh 11
Hours: not listed
Phone: 732 160 647
Tram: 2, 9, 18, 22 and 23 to Národní Třída
Metro: Yellow ("B") line to Národní Třída
Email: adgalerie@seznam.cz

Michalská Street

As was mentioned previously, this street has been filled with art galleries for some years now. Though not as many have survived to the present day as there were when this phenomenon first came about, it is still a good place to look for art.

You can also find local artists selling their work on the Charles Bridge and at **Havel's Market** (see "Outdoor Markets"). And the

Malá Strana (Lesser Quarter) tends to have small art galleries sprinkled throughout it, especially on Nerudova Street and just under and around the Charles Bridge.

AD Galerie

ART SUPPLIES

A town with artists needs art supplies, of course. Prague has some unique places in this area.

Koh-i-Noor Hardtmuth

I'm guessing that you probably didn't know that this world leader in art supplies has resided in the Bohemian town of České Budějovice since 1848 (the company was founded in Vienna in 1790). Koh-i-Noor produces a full range of artists' materials, from paper to pastels, but is it famous for its mechanical and graphite lead pencils which have won many awards over the years.

Koh-i-Noor's website features some interesting trivia about the company:

- It's founder, Josef Hardtmuth, invented the modern graphite pencil, and their production process is still the same today as that developed by Hardtmuth;
- The graphite pencil called "KOH-I-NOOR" and marked "1500" is the most popular pencil in the world;
- The current world standard of marking gradations of lead's softness or hardness with numbers and the letters HB or F originated at the factory in České Budějovice.

While Koh-i-Noor products have been available for years in shops and department stores around the country, more recently the company has begun opening its own retail stores. Their products, especially a mechanical pencil for the engineering grad on your list, make great gifts and/or souvenirs.

Koh-i-Noor

Na Příkopě 26
Hours: daily 10:00 – 20:00
Phone: 739 329 019
Tram: 6, 8, 15, 26 to Náměstí Republiky
Yellow ("B") line to Náměstí Republiky
www.koh-i-noor.cz

Koh-i-noor Stationary
Nerudova 13
Hours: daily 10:00 – 19:00
Phone: 731 534 401
Tram: 12, 15, 20, 22 or 23 to Malostranské Náměstí

Zlatá Loď

Zlatá Lod' is probably the best and the largest art supply store in Prague. In this locally-owned institution, you're sure to find exactly what you're looking for, or something unique that you can't get in the U.S. or elsewhere. Especially when it comes to oil paints, you will definitely find some colors and brands that will be new to you and fun to experiment with. It's conveniently located in Old Town in the Platýz courtyard off of Národní.

Zlatá Lod'
Národní 37
Hours: Mon.-Fri. 9.00 – 19.00, Sat. 10:00 – 17.00, closed Sunday
Phone: 222 220 174
Tram: 2, 9, 18, 22 or 23 to Národní Třída
Metro: Yellow ("B") line to Národní Třída
www.zlatalod.cz

51

9 BOOKS AND ANTIQUARIAN SHOPS

There are a few English-language bookshops in Prague, all with very good selections, especially considering their relatively small size. The offerings also include lots of local interest books and works by Czech authors translated into English. In addition, many Czech bookshops have English language sections of varying degrees of quality and size. Here are some places to check out.

The Globe Bookstore & Cafe

The Globe was the first English-language bookshop in Prague and was quite the hangout for the expat crowd (especially the Americans among us) when it first opened over in the Holešovice neighborhood back in the early 90s. Now it's more conveniently located in New Town, a few blocks behind the National Theater. The Globe features a wide range of titles, a cozy atmosphere and not bad food and coffee in the café.

The Globe Bookstore & Cafe
Pštrossova 6
Hours: Mon.-Fri. 10:00 – midnight, Sat.-Sun.9:30 – 1:00 a.m.
Phone: 224 934 203
Tram: 5 to Myslíkova
www.globebookstore.cz/

The Globe interior

Shakespeare & Sons

Located in Malá Strana, this little shop is one of Prague's two remaining English-language bookshops and manages to maintain a rather extensive, high-quality selection of English language books (as well as a lot of fairly-cheap used books, in case you need to pick something up for that flight home or a train ride to Berlin). You might even see a few of my books for sale at Shakespeare!

Shakespeare & Sons interior

Shakespeare and Sons Bookshop

U Lužického Semináře 10
Hours: daily 11:00 – 21:00
Phone: 257 531 894
Tram: 12, 15, 20, 22 or 23 to Malostranské Náměstí
Metro: Green ("A") line to Malostranská
www.shakes.cz

The Franz Kafka Society

The Franz Kafka Society is a non-profit that was established in 1990 to devote *"systematic attention to [Kafka's] works, seeking to make Kafka's heritage a natural component of the Czech cultural context,"* according to its website. In my view, this is both a necessary and worthy task – Kafka was all but ignored by the communists, who never could decide if his work supported their ideology or not.

In addition to a replica of Kafka's library, a publishing house, and the Franz Kafka Prize, the Society also has a bookshop in the front of its headquarters where you can find the works of Kafka, of course, as well as many titles connected to Central Europe by Czech and other authors.

The Franz Kafka Society z.s.

Široká 14
Hours: daily 10:00 – 18:00
Phone.: 224 227 452 (secretariat), 739 331 782
Tram: 2, 17 or 18 to Staroměstská
Metro: Green ("A") line to Staroměstská
E-mail: mail@franzkafka-soc.cz
www.franzkafka-soc.cz

NeoLuxor

This chain of bookstores is the Czech Republic's largest, both in terms of number of stores and breadth of selection. Of course, most of their books are in the Czech language, but the shops all have well-stocked English language sections, as well as plenty of books that are available only in the English language, such as international art books, in other sections. Even the smaller branches have a decent selection of books in English, but the flagship store on Wenceslas Square has the largest (located on the lower level), with the branch in the Palladium shopping mall running a close second. And NeoLuxor now has a store at Prague's main train station, so you can pick up something to read on your trip to your next destination! The main Wenceslas Square location is listed below. See their website for other listings.

NeoLuxor - Palác Knih Luxor (Luxor Palace of Books)
Václavské Náměstí 41
Hours: vary by location
Tram: 3, 5, 6, 9, 14, or 24 to Václavské Náměstí
Metro: Green ("A") or Yellow ("B") line to Můstek
www.neoluxor.cz/pobocky/praha

Book Therapy

This shop really tries to live up to its name with its very eclectic selection of unique titles on everything from design to travel to fashion and fiction. Book Therapy's sleek, uncluttered design is also a pleasing to the eye and soul. Such a one-of-a-kind collection under one roof certainly won't be found in any other bookstore in Prague – and probably not anywhere else. A visit to Book Therapy requires a metro or tram ride to Vinohrady, so you might want to combine it with porcelain shopping if you're considering a visit to Dům Porcelánu (See "Crystal, Fine Glass & Porcelain") or with antique shopping on Korunní.

Book Therapy
Římská 35
Hours: Mon.-Fri. 12:00 – 20:00, Sat. 11:00 – 16:00
Phone: 603 524 782
Tram: 4, 10, 16 and 22 to Náměstí Míru
Metro: Green ("A) line to Náměstí Míru
www.booktherapy.cz

Book Therapy entrance

ANTIQUARIAN SHOPS

Unfortunately, there aren't many of these old map, print and book shops left in the center of town, and even the ones further out in the suburbs are also disappearing. But there are a couple left that you can check out:

Antikvariát Valentinská

This is one of the better antikvariáts still hanging on.

Antikvariát Valentinská

Valentinská 8
Hours: Mon.-Fri. 10:00 – 18:00, closed Saturday and Sunday
Phone: 224 816 253

Antikvariát & Galerie

This one is just around the corner from Antikvariát Valentinská, and it is notable for its large collection of nice prints.

Antikvariát & Galerie

Veleslavínova 3
No other information listed

10 DESIGN, SPECIALTY AND GIFT SHOPS

One needs only to observe the classic Czech trams to realize that Czech design is truly unique. The architecture of Prague shows that both beauty and a flare for the unusual has always run through Czech creativity. There are many design shops sprinkled throughout Prague, and several design festivals and marketplaces happen throughout the year, as well. And not just Czech items can be found – Prague now has many shops selling unique design items from elsewhere.

In addition to the design stores listed here, Vinohradská Street in the heart of the trendy Vinohrady neighborhood has morphed into a kind of "design street." Much of the lower part of it – from just behind the National Museum at the top of Wenceslas Square up to Šumavská Street – is lined with home décor and design shops of all kinds. The Vinohradský Pavilon at the corner of Šumavská is a former 19th-century marketplace that became one of the city's first shopping malls after the Velvet Revolution. Now the entire thing has been turned into a design market that has some really interesting shops and brands. So if you have time to head to Vinohrady and are interested in chic, sleek European design, it might be worth a trip. Otherwise, here are some places in the city center for you to check out:.

Classic Czech-made tram from the early 1960s – still in action!
Reprinted with permission from Pixabay CC

Kubista

Located in one of the few Cubist-style buildings in Old Town (the House of the Black Madonna), Kubista carries a unique selection of mainly Cubist and Art Deco decorative items and design pieces. These reproductions are mostly based on originals from early twentieth-century applied art designs and motifs. I especially love the Czech Cubist ceramic pieces.

After shopping, you can quench your thirst or satisfy your sweet tooth in the Grand Orient Café on the second floor that is still decorated in its original Cubist-period style. See my **"Prague Restaurant Guide"** or my **Old Town walk** in the Chapter titled "Contact Me" for more information on the House of the Black Madonna and café.

Kubista
Ovocný Trh 19
Hours: Tue.-Sun. 10:00 – 18:30, closed Monday
Phone: 224 236 378
Tram: 6, 8, 15, 26 to Náměstí Republiky

Metro: Yellow ("B") line to Náměstí Republiky
Bus: 207 to Náměstí Republiky
www.kubista.cz/en/

Kubista in the House of the Black Madonna

Lípa

The name means "linden," like the tree, and Lípa is the newest line of Czech handcrafted products. Their motto is "Gifts with a Czech touch. And Love." Their selection, which leans toward the trendy and modern with a nod to the traditional, ranges from food products (pear jam and plum sauce) to porcelain and leather-bound journals, all decorated with graphics of the linden blossom or leaf. While their products are available in several shops (See Book Therapy in "Books and Antiquarian Shops"), Lípa recently opened its own shop in Old Town on Malé Náměstí, just off of Old Town Square.

Lípa
Malé Náměstí 4
Hours: daily 11:00 – 20:00

Phone: 602 557 598
Tram: 2, 17 or 18 to Staroměstská
Metro: Green ("A") line to Staroměstská
www.lipastore.cz

Naoko

Naoko 1 & 2

Naoko has two shops next to each other that carry designer household gadgets and gifts, especially unusual brands. Think the Sharper Image for kitchen gadgets and housewares. You'll surely find something to surprise and to please here.

Naoko 1 & 2
Revoluční 24
Hours: Mon.-Fri. 10:00 – 18:00, closed Saturday and Sunday
Phone: 222 312 567
Tram: 6, 8, 15 and 26 to Dlouhá Třída
Metro: Yellow ("B") line to Náměstí Republiky
Bus: 207 to Dlouhá Třída
www.naoko.cz

Pod 7 Kilo (Under 7 Kilos)

If you're someone who can't resist gadgets or those "why didn't I think of that?" objects or items that fill needs you didn't think could be met or needs you didn't know you had, stay away from this shop unless you want to spend all of your money. Actually, it doesn't fill all needs – just the travel kind – and it does a great job of it. I guarantee you'll find a lot of things here you didn't know existed, and more than once you'll say to yourself, "Oh, I could use one of those!"

Actually, the shop is very small, because every item must weigh less than 7 kilos, so that might help save your wallet. Seriously, though, you will enjoy even just browsing in this store.

Pod 7 Kilo (Under 7 Kilos)
Rybná 26
Hours: Mon.-Thu. 10:00 – 18:00, Fri. 10:00 – 17:00 (break from 12:30 – 13:30 Mon.-Fri.), Sat. 10:00 – 14:00
Phone: 211 221 829
Tram: 6, 8, 26 to Dlouhá Třída

Metro: Yellow ("B") line to Náměstí Republiky
Bus: 207 to Dlouhá Třída
www.pod7kilo.cz

Hefaistos entrance

Hefaistos

Traditional blacksmiths are a bit of a rarity in today's modern world, but this one in Prague's Old Town makes some beautiful products – from small door knockers and handles that you can take home to large suits of armor. You can also find their blacksmiths working at the market on Náměstí Republiky on weekdays.

Hefaistos
Rybná 21
Hours: Not listed
Phone: 602 295 500
Email: obchod@hefaistospraha.cz
www.hefaistospraha.cz/index.php/en

Christmas Ornament Shop at Prague Castle

The only name I have ever seen on this shop is "Christmas Ornaments." And that's exactly what it is. It's tiny but is crammed full of all kinds and sizes of beautiful Christmas ornaments year-round. Almost all of them are Czech and are hand-made, including many beautiful glass ornaments. So if you're a Christmas person – or even if you're not – check out this shop. These ornaments make nice souvenirs to take home. Don't worry – they pack them well in bubble wrap.

The shop is located on Jiřská Street within the Prague Castle complex. Jiřská is the street that runs from St. George's Basilica toward the Golden Lane (Zlatá Ulička) and the Old Castle Steps (Staré Zámecké Schody). When you see the sign pointing toward the Golden Lane, the shop is just ahead of you on the left-hand side of the street with the basilica behind you.

Christmas Shop at Prague Castle
Jiřská Street
Prague Castle district

Hunter-Just Your Friend

Designer sweaters and fancy bowls and beds for your dog? You bet! If you love your pet, make a visit to this high-end shop for pet accessories and pick out a present for your pooch.

Hunter-Just Your Friend

Újezd 35
Hours: daily 10:00 – 21:00
Phone: 777 802 421
Tram: 12, 15, 20, 22 or 23 to Hellichova
Metro: Green ("A") line to Malostranská
www.justhunter.cz/en

Hunter-Just Your Friend entrance

FotoŠkoda

Take my word for it: photographers and camera and gadget lovers will not want to miss this shop. Occupying several levels of a building near Wenceslas Square, FotoŠkoda has everything you could need or want relating to photography – including film and the cameras that use them for those who have resisted the pull to switch to digital. And they are experts. Their staff knows all there is to know about the products they sell, and they will most likely know all there is to know about the apparatus you're using to capture images of Prague. Should you have a problem with or question about that new camera you bought for your trip, stop by and they will help you sort it out. And it's fun just browsing through (or gawking at?) the wide range of devices they carry.

FotoŠkoda
Vodičkova 37
Hours: Mon.-Fri. 9:00 – 19:00, Sat.-Sun. 11:00 – 18:00
Phone: 222 929 029
Tram: 3, 5, 6, 9, 14, 24 to Václavské Náměstí
Metro: Green ("A") line to Můstek (exit in the direction of Vodičkova Street)
www.fotoskoda.cz

Flying Tiger

If you like the types of gadgets and knickknacks found at Naoko, you'll probably like Flying Tiger, too. Hailing from Denmark, these shops are a mecca for anyone looking for that small little gift or object that you didn't know you wanted (and probably don't need). In any case, Flying Tiger's products fascinate and cover almost every aspect of life. Prague has several stores, and I list the Old Town location here. Others can be found on Flying Tiger's website:

Flying Tiger
Rytířská 29
Hours: daily 9:00 – 21:00
Phone: 727 865 111
Metro: Green ("A") line to Můstek
https://cz.flyingtiger.com/cs-CZ/

Bohemia Paper (J. Orb Paper Shop)

If you love paper, you'll love this shop. But it's not just paper –
Bohemia Paper by J. Orb is preserving the art of hand-engraved
cards and envelopes. These finely crafted products make great gifts
or mementos: They're small, relatively light-weight and unique,
and they won't break. Pick up a pack of monogrammed greeting
cards, some table place cards for your next dinner party, or some
beautifully decorated birthday or Christmas cards with Prague
motifs.

Bohemia Paper entrance

Bohemia Paper (J Orb Paper Shop)
Palác Kinských (Kinsky Palace)
Hours: Mon.-Fri. 10:00 – 18:00, Sat.-Sun.11:00 – 18:00
Phone: 266 712 566
Tram: 2, 17 or 18 to Staroměstská
Metro: Green ("A") line to Staroměstská
Bus: 194 to Masná
www.bohemiapaper.cz

Moleskin interior

Moleskin

While both ubiquitous and famous in the US for some time, Moleskin became available in Prague only a few years ago, first appearing in a retail store dedicated solely to the brand. Subsequently the notebooks have also become available in bookshops and other retail outlets, but even so, it's kind of fun to see a whole shop full of just about every type of notebook the company has to offer.

Moleskin

Bělehradská 70
Hours: Mon.-Fri. 12:00-19:00, closed Sat.-Sun.
Phone: 724 306 565
Tram: 6, 11, 13 to Bruselská or 4, 6, 10, 11, 13, 16, 22 to I.P. Pavlova
www.moleskine.cz/

Papelote

When it comes to paper and notebooks, Papelote is a paper lover's paradise (and maybe a writer's paradise also). These environmentally-friendly, Czech-made cards and notebooks are one of a kind.

Papelote

Vojtěšská 9
Hours: Mon.-Fri. 11:00 – 19:00, Sat. 12:00–18:00
Phone: 774 719 113
Tram: 5 to Jiráskovo Náměstí
Email: info@papelote.cz
www.papelote.eu

CUBAN CIGARS

If you decide you'd like to smoke a few genuine Cuban cigars while you're in Prague, there are a couple of humidors you can check out: One is the Cigar Club at La Bodeguita del Medio on Kaprova Street and the other is La Casa del Habano on Dlouhá Street, which runs off of the other side of Old Town Square. I have no idea what will happen if you try to take them back to the U.S. and the customs agent finds them (though the restrictions may be loosening?). So, I'll leave that up to you. But you can smoke them here with no problem.

La Bodeguita del Medio
Kaprova 5
Hours: Sun.-Tue. 11:00-2:00 a.m., Wed. – Sat. 11:00 – 4:00 a.m.
Phone: 224 813 922
Tram: 2, 17, 18 to Staroměstská
Metro: Green ("A") line to Staroměstská
Bus: 194 to Staroměstská
www.labodeguitadelmedio.cz

La Casa del Argentina
Dlouhá 35
Hours: Sun.-Mon. 11:30 – 1:00 a.m., Tue.-Sat. 11:30 – 2:00 a.m.
Phone: 222 311 512
Tram: 6, 8, 15 and 26 to Dlouhá Třída
Metro: Yellow ("B") line to Náměstí Republiky
Bus: 194 to Hradební
www.lacasaargentina.cz

11 GOURMET FOOD SHOPS AND GROCERY STORES

My **Prague restaurant guide** explores the food revolution happening in Prague currently, and that revolution has resulted in the bourgeoning of artisanal food shops throughout the city. They've opened everywhere from the center of town to the suburbs and in shopping malls, too. They feature a mix of gourmet Czech and imported items, both fresh and preserved. Some of the best ones are listed below (but there are many more!). I've also listed some regular grocery stores in case you are self-catering in an Airbnb or other rental apartment

DelMart

The founder of this chain of small, accessible shops had a former life as the buyer for the Czech Republic's Marks & Spencer grocery stores. Armed with the knowledge gleaned in that job, he set out to provide gourmet groceries to the Czech market at more affordable prices than M&S. He seems to have succeeded, and DelMarts are now sprouting up all over the city. The locals tend to like this store a lot.

You'll find DelMart locations at Anděl, near the northern

entrance to the Anděl metro station; in the Quadrio behind My/Tesco at the Národní Třída metro and tram stops; and near the Marriott Hotel on V Celnici. Featuring a wide variety of beautiful fresh fruits and vegetables, good cheeses and meats, DelMart also has such novelties (for Prague, at least) as gourmet root beer and genuine maple syrup. The prices here tend to be a bit more reasonable than at some of the other gourmet shops, and DelMart also has more local Czech products than many of the others. The larger DelMart locations have eat-in bistros.

DelMart
V Celnici 10, Praha 1
Hours: Mon.-Fri. 7.00 – 22.00, Sat.-Sun. 8.00 – 22.00
Phone: 735 174 707 (Bistro), 735 755 831 (Shop)
Email: prodejna.millennium@delmart.cz
www.delmart.cz/

One of many new DelMart locations

Food Story

This is another addition to Prague's list of gourmet food shops, having opened in late 2014. Food Story conveniently located just off of Old Town Square at Dlouhá 14 (the entrance is actually on Masná Street, but if you walk down Dlouhá with Old Town Square at your back, you'll find it on the right just after Dlouhá forks). This grocery store's focus is having an assortment of high quality Czech and imported products. Inside you'll find not only an exotic range of fruits and vegetables, but also a coffee bar with Italian pastries (great cannoli) from the Moje Kredenc chain that a few years ago opened shops with quality Italian products in many of Prague's suburban shopping malls.

Next to the grocery store you'll find the "Rybárna" (fish market) full of many types of fresh fish and seafood. You can buy your fish to take home or have it cooked by the chefs on hand and eat it on the spot, another popular trend in many gourmet food shops in Prague these days.

Food Story
Dlouhá 14
Hours: daily 9:00 – midnight
Phone: 607 940 605
Tram: 6, 8, 15, or 26 to Dlouhá Třída
Bus: 194 to Masná
www.foodstory.cz

Gourmet Pasáž Dlouhá

Prague is filled with passages ("pasáž") that locals in the know use to beat the crowds and save time by cutting from one area of town to the next in a more direct fashion than the city's medieval street plan allows. But the Dlouhá pasáž is the first one whose shops have been dedicated entirely to one theme, and that theme is food. The star here is probably Naše Maso, a butcher shop that is part of the Ambiente restaurant group and is also the meat supplier to that group's restaurants. Naše Maso has all kinds of quality beef and pork products – fresh, aged, smoked or cured. You can select a fresh steak or hamburger patty, and, as at the Rybárna, have it expertly grilled to your liking for immediate consumption, or take it home to cook for yourself.

A Vietnamese restaurant in the Dlouhá Pasáž

Other notable shops in this pasáž include a chocolatier (Chocotherapia), a wine bar, and a snack bar called Sisters. Sisters is run by Hana Michopulu, author of the well-known cookbooks *Zpátky Domů (Back Home Again)* and *Recepty z Farmářského Trhu (Recipes from the Farmer's Market)*, and features modern versions of Czech "lahůdky" (snacks or refreshments), including the classic "chlebíčky" (open-faced sandwiches topped with ham, cheese, egg, tomato, onion and more). Czechs are crazy about chlebíčky, and the modern variations at Sisters are really good.

Gourmet Pasáž Dlouhá
Dlouhá 39
Hours: Shop hours vary
Tram: 6, 8, 15, or 26 to Dlouhá Třída
www.gurmetpasazdlouha.eu/en

La Bottega

This is a chain of bistros and Italian delicatessens belonging to the La Finestra restaurant group. There are four in town, including this one in the Gourmet Pasáž Dlouhá (and one next to La Finestra on Platneřská). La Bottega features prosciutto, pasta, cheeses and fine wine. Eat in, take out or do your grocery shopping. They also have a reasonably-priced Sunday brunch.

La Bottega
Dlouhá 39
Hours: Mon.-Sat. 9:00 – 24:00 (kitchen until 22:30), Sun. 9:00 – 22:00 (kitchen until 21:00)
Phone: 222 311 372
Tram: 6, 8, 15, or 26 to Dlouhá Třída
www.labottega.cz

WineFood Market

This Italian grocery and wine shop also has a food court serving everything from pizza to lasagna and a café that serves great coffee in the Smíchov neighborhood (Prague 5). Note that there is a second Prague location in the Dejvice neighborhood (without a food court).

WineFood Market
Strakonická 1
Hours: Mon.-Sat. 7:00 – 23:00, Sun. 8:00 – 23:00 (kitchen from 11:30 to 22:00)
Phone: 733 338 650
Tram: 4, 12, 15 or 20 to Plzeňka (all of these trams can be found at the Anděl metro and tram stations)
Email: info@winemarket.cz
www.winemarket.cz

Tesco

This is a British department store that can satisfy all of your practical and grocery needs. The building on Národní, which formerly housed the communist-era "Máj" department store, recently underwent a major renovation and facelift, and the interior is now quite appealing. One of the best additions was a Costa

Coffee shop (a British imitation of Starbucks) on the ground floor in the rear, in case you need a refreshment break when you hop off the 22 tram on your way back from Malá Strana or Prague Castle. For the summer months, a new terrace restaurant and grill located on the roof offers a different view of this part of Prague. Also called "My/Tesco."

My Tesco Národní
Národní 26
Hours: Mon.-Sat. 7:00 - 21:00; Sunday and holidays 8:00 - 21:00
Phone: 222 815 111
Tram: 2, 9, 18, 22 or 23 to Národní Třída:
Metro: Yellow ("B") line to Národní Třída
www.mystores.cz

Tesco at Anděl
Radlická 1/b
Hours: daily 6:00 – 24:00
Phone: 257 284 371
Tram: 4, 5, 6, 7, 9, 10, 12, 15, 16, or 20 to Anděl
Metro: Anděl
www.itesco.cz

Albert

A Dutch chain, Albert grocery stores are sprinkled throughout the city. In the historic area of town you will find an Albert in the Palladium Shopping Center on Náměstí Republiky and one across the street in front of the Kotva department store. You'll also find one in the Můstek metro station at Wenceslas Square and another on Rytířská Street at number 10, not too far away from Old Town Square.

www.albert.cz

Billa

Billa is an Austrian grocery chain, and the largest Billa in the center of town is in Celnice just around the corner from Náměstí Republiky. Another one can be found near the Hilton Pobřežní in the passage leading from the hotel parking lot to the Florenc tram and metro stations. In New Town, you'll find a Billa store on the western side of Karlovo Náměstí (Charles Square). And very conveniently, Billa recently opened a store in Prague's main train station, Hlavní Nádraží.

Marks & Spencer

In addition to these traditional grocery stores, Marks & Spencer in the Czech Republic has now included groceries in all of its Prague stores. They are considerably pricier than the "ordinary" grocery stores listed above, but the quality of many of the fresh products is noticeably better, and they have a more interesting selection of goods in general. M&S also features some pre-prepared meals that need only heating up.

Marks & Spencer can be found on Wencelsas Square (at number 36), in the Palladium on Náměstí Republiky, and in the Anděl shopping mall at the Anděl metro and tram stops.

http://global.marksandspencer.com/cz/

12 HEALTH AND BEAUTY

Some unique local producers of organic and natural cosmetics have hit the Prague market, and one can also find international products that might not be widely available in the US and elsewhere. Here are a few selections:

Botanicus

These shops sell hand-made soaps, shampoos, oils, etc., and actually grow the ingredients for their products on their own farm in the Czech countryside.

Botanicus products make good gifts to take back home – unlike the glass and crystal, most of these products won't break, are small and can be packed easily in your luggage. The main store is located in Týnský Dvůr just off of Old Town Square.

Botanicus Prague - Ungelt
Týn 3 (Týnský Dvůr, also called Ungelt)
Hours: daily 10:00 – 20:00
Phone: 234 767 446
Email: praha.ungelt@botanicus.cz
www.botanicus.cz/en

Dr. Hauschka

A pioneer in the area of natural skin treatments and cosmetics who was once imprisoned by the Nazis, Dr. Rudolf Hauschka (with the help of cosmetologist Elisabeth Sigmund) developed natural cosmetics and skin creams that don't contain chemical/synthetic emulsifiers or alcohol as preservatives. His products are still widely sought today, and Prague has a Dr. Hauschka retail outlet on the border between Old and New Towns on Revoluční Street.

Dr. Hauschka
Revoluční 10
Hours: Mon.-Fri. 10:00 – 19:00, Sat. 11:00 – 16:00, closed Sunday
Phone: 233 320 249
Tram: 6, 8, 15 and 26 to Dlouhá Třída
Metro: Yellow ("B") line to Náměstí Republiky
Bus: 207 to Dlouhá Třída

See also Manufaktura under "Marionettes, Handicrafts and Toys."

Country Life

In the early 1990s, this was the first (and for many years the only) health food store in Prague. It also has a vegetarian restaurant attached that also serves a lot of vegan dishes. The Melantrichova shop location offering a variety of fresh and packaged organic products is close to Old Town Square. Their organic cosmetics store is not far away on Liliová Street.

Country Life
Melantrichova 15
Hours: Mon.-Thu. 8:30 – 19:00, Fri. 8:30 – 16:30, Sun. 11:00 – 18:00, closed Saturday
Phone: 224 213 366
Metro: Green ("A") line to Můstek
Email: melantrichova@countrylife.cz
www.countrylife.cz

Organic and Natural Cosmetics
Liliová 11
Hours: Mon.-Thu. 9:00–19:00, Fr 9:00 – 16:30, closed Sat.-Sun.
Phone: 230 233 860
Tram: 2, 17 or 18 to Karlovy Lázně
Email: kosmetika@countrylife.cz

13 HOME, HOUSEWARES AND KITCHEN

Prague has a couple of standout shops in this area. My favorites are listed here.

Le Patio

This shop, opened in the early 1990s by a Belgian expatriate, was at the time of its founding the only place in town where one could find decent gifts and home décor items. Such was the situation at that time in Prague that when gifts were exchanged on birthdays, my friends and I would open one package after another that had come from Le Patio, and the homes of just about all of my friends in the expat community were decorated with Le Patio items (until they were all decorated with items from Ikea and then progressed from there). Now that there's plenty of choice on the market, Le Patio is still an old favorite because of the attractiveness and uniqueness of its products.

The new flagship shop at Jungmannova 30 in New Town is not only a great place to shop or browse, but the building in which it's located (the Mozarteum) is an exceptional example of 1920s Art Deco architecture by renowned Czech architect Jan Kotěra.

Le Patio
Dušní 8
Hours: Mon.-Sat. 10:00 – 19:00. Sun. 11:00 – 19:00
Phone: 224 934 402
Tram: 16 to Pravnická Fakulta
Metro: Green ("A") line to Staroměstská
Bus: 194 to Masná
www.lepatio.cz

Le Patio interior

Potten & Pannen

If you love kitchen gadgets and housewares, you'll love the "purely Czech" Potten & Pannen, as it describes itself. Founded in 1992 when not only was there really nothing that could compare in Prague, but really nothing at all in its market niche, Potten & Pannen had a bold vision per its website:

> *"To elevate cooking, dining and everything ... [in] the kitchen to a paramount art. To put the perfect tools from... the world's best brands into the hands of both experienced professionals and enthusiastic amateurs ...."*

A visit to one of their stores will show that they've done a pretty good job. Though the electric appliances won't work for those of you living in the US or some other countries, it's still fun to look. And there are plenty of non-electric gadgets and other items that you can use anywhere.

Potten & Pannen interior

Potten & Pannen

Újezd 25
Hours: Mon.-Fri. 9:00 – 19:00, Sat. 9:00 – 18:00, closed Sunday
Phone: 222 232 525
Tram: 12, 15, 20, 22 or 23 to Hellichova
www.pottenpannen.cz/en/

14 LUXURY SHOPPING

Without a doubt, there's only one place to head when it comes to luxury brands: Pařížská (Paris) Street in Old Town. Cutting through what once was the heart of the old Jewish Quarter, Pařížská Street was the premier address in a 19th-century gentrification project. The street is lined with some of the most beautiful buildings in Prague, and many would say that it's the most beautiful street in the city.

The apartment buildings on Pařížská were always luxurious and meant for the wealthy, and **since the Velvet Revolution of 1989 its beautiful storefronts have been home to the world's top luxury fashion brands.** But in the early 90s, these shops couldn't sustain themselves in a country with a post-communist economy where the average salary was about the equivalent of $100 a month (and in a city that was not yet discovered by tourists with hard currency to spend). So, a shop would open and then close a few months later. Then another luxury brand would move into the space, and, inevitably, the initial brand that had failed would try again a year or so later in a different building – but always on Pařížská Street. Eventually the market stabilized, and Pařížská Street has for several years now been the premier address for luxury shopping in Prague.

The apartments above have also been turned into luxury homes, and the tree-lined street on which they stand (trees being a rarity in medieval Old Town, but this street having been built in the 19th century allowed for more modern street planning) is a pleasant one for outdoor dining, strolling, window-shopping or real shopping if your bank account can take it. And due to the income level of the street's residents, Pařížská is also a great place for car spotting.

Here are some of the stores and brands you'll find on Pařížská:

- Tiffany
- Hermes
- Jimmy Choo
- Kosta Boda
- Louis Vuitton
- Cartier
- Prada
- Gucci
- Patek Philippe
- Vertu
- Rolex

To find a list of all the shops and services on Pařížská Street, check out this website:

www.parizskaulice.cz

15 MUSIC AND MUSICAL INSTRUMENTS

As I mentioned in the chapter on Prague history, the Baroque Counter-Reformation building boom not only gave Prague some beautiful architecture and art – it also turned its population into extremely musically-literate music lovers. You'll notice that there are concerts everywhere every day throughout Prague, and the nation boasts a world-class orchestra in the Czech Philharmonic. So naturally, the city of Prague features lots of shops selling music, musical instruments and concert tickets. Check these out when you're here:

Via Musica

While Via Musica's main activity is acting as a ticket portal for classical and jazz concerts in Prague, it's also the best CD shop in the city for both of those genres with a selection of over 3,500 CDs to choose from.

According to their website, Via Musica *"... has become the hot destination for many musicians, music experts and fans of classical music and jazz. [We] carry a wide selection of Czech and international classical music from all periods to modern, contemporary classics and Czech jazz. [Via Musica] has been awarded the prestigious "retailer of the year" award by*

Supraphon, the leading publisher of classical music in the Czech Republic since 2005."

If you're a classical or jazz music fan who would enjoy picking up a hard-to-find CD, stop by this shop just off of Old Town Square, in a small alley next to the Týn Church (as you face the church, the alley is just to the left of it).

Via Musica
Staroměstské Náměstí 14
Hours: daily 10:00 – 20:00 (closes at 18:00 November – March)
Phone: 224 826 440
Tram: 2, 17 or 18 to Staroměstská
Metro: Green ("A") line to Staroměstská
Bus: 194 to Masná
www.viamusica.cz/en/

MUSICAL INSTRUMENTS

Like antiques and "antikvariats," quaint little shops selling musical instruments of all kinds used to be rather common in Prague, especially in the Old Town. Now we're down to a few, and I hope they manage to stay around. Here's a selection:

Hudební Nástroje Radek Bubrle (Radek Bubrle Musical Instruments)

This is one of the few traditional musical instruments shops left in Prague. Mr. Bubrle's shop carries new and used instruments, from banjos and accordions to violins.

Hudební Nástroje Radek Bubrle
Náprstkova
Hours: Mon.-Fri. 10:00 – 18:00, Sat. 10:00 – 16:00, closed Sunday
Phone: 222 221 100
Tram: 17 or 18 to Karlovy Lázně
www.nastroje-hudebni.cz/

Via Musica entrance in the lane next to the Týn Church

Hudební Nástroje "U Zlatého Kohouta" (Musical Instruments at the Golden Rooster)

This is another rare traditional musical instrument shop that is still hanging on in Old Town and is quite near Hudební Nástroje Radek Bubrle.

Hudební Nástroje "U Zlatého Kohouta"

Michalská 3
Hours: Mon.-Thu. 10:00 – 12:00 and 13:00 – 18:00, Fri. 10:00 – 12:00 and 13:00 – 18:00, closed Saturday and Sunday
Phone: 224 212 874
Tram: 2, 9, 18, 22 or 23 to Národní Třída
Metro: Yellow ("B") line to Národní Třída

Houslařský Atelier Vávra entrance

Houslařský Atelier Vávra (Vávra Violin Studio)

It's rare to see a violin shop these days, but this one in the Vinohrady neighborhood is as quaint as you would picture it to be.

Houslařský Atelier Vávra

Lublaňská 65
Phone: 222 518 114, 728 040 214
Hours: Mon.-Fri. 9:00 – 17:00
Email: houslar.vavra@quick.cz
Tram: 4, 6, 10, 16, 22 and 23 to I.P. Pavlova
Metro: Red ("C") line to I.P. Pavlova
www.housle-vavra.cz/en/index.php

VINYL RECORDS

Prague is not short of "vinyl culture," and if you're into it, too, then there are several shops you might want to check out. In addition to the records from international artists that are on sale here, the Czech Republic has one of the few vinyl producers left in the world, and their business has been booming in recent years.

A New York Times article titled *Czech Company, Pressing Hits for Years on Vinyl, Finds It Has Become One* (Lyman, 2015) tells the story of the company's success, while another on The Vinyl Factory website touts the success of the largest quality turntable manufacturer in the world – which happens to be in the Czech Republic: *The world's biggest quality turntable maker sees production soar 400%* (Spice, 2017).

I'm not sure if the turntables will work in your home country, but if you've got a functioning one at home, you can pick up some records at the following shops:

Phono.cz

Most people in town consider this to be the best vinyl shop in Prague. This small store has both new and used records, and the staff knows their selection well. Check it out if you're looking for a hard-to-find album.

Phono.cz
Opatovická 24
Hours: Mon.-Fri. 13:00 – 19:00 (Closed December 24 - January 2)
Phone: 222 521 448
Tram: 2, 9, 18, 22 or 23 to Národní Třída:
Metro: Yellow ("B") line to Národní Třída
Email: eshop@phono.cz
www.phono.cz

Happyfeet Vinyl Record Shop Prague

This is another good place to check out. It's run by Magdalena

Happyfeet, the Vinyl Queen.

Happyfeet Vinyl Record Shop Prague
Vodičkova 36 (in the Lucerna Passage)
Hours: Mon.-Fri. 12:30 – 19:00
Phone: 606 722 655
Email: magdalena@happyfeet.cz
www.happyfeet.cz

16 OUTDOOR MARKETS

When I first moved here, outdoor markets were not very prevalent, and those that did exist were nothing to write home about. As was mentioned in the Introduction to this book, having a variety of goods available was not a hallmark of communism. The Czech Republic's weather (cold much of the year) and relative lack of fresh indigenous fruits and vegetables also contributed to the lack of markets. The best market at that time was Havel's Market, but it still was lacking in availability and variety when compared with the markets found in warmer (and non-communist) places like France or Italy.

These days the situation has improved, especially with the addition of farmer's markets (and Easter and Christmas markets at the appropriate times). But the farmer's markets are closed in the winter months, and they still don't have the variety typical of markets found in warmer climes. But they are good enough – and not just for the fruits and vegetables on sale, but for the grilled meats, beer, coffee and sweets also available, making them real social gathering places as well, especially when the weather's nice. Here are some markets that are fun to visit:

Havelské Tržíště (Havel's Market)

This is one of Prague's oldest marketplaces and is located on a site that **has served as a market for centuries.** When I first moved to Prague, Havel's Market had mostly fruit and vegetable stands with a few flower sellers thrown in. Now, the fruit and vegetable stands have shrunk to a pitiful few, while rather junkie souvenirs have taken over most of the space.

Havel's Market

However, there are a few decent photographs and paintings (careful – some are originals and some are prints) for sale, and some of the souvenirs aren't bad either, like hand-painted Prague-themed bookmarks or refrigerator magnets. So, you might be able to pick up a few small and easy-to-pack gifts for friends here, and there's always a Prague tee-shirt or beer stein for your teenager or college student (respectively).

Beware of the highly overpriced and artfully pre-arranged fresh fruit baskets, complete with a small plastic fork for street consumption by unsuspecting tourists. You will pay an arm and a leg for these beautiful treats. The trick is that they are price by 100 grams and not by the kilo like the other fruits and vegetables on offer.

Havelské Tržíště

Havelská Street at the corner of Melantrichova in Old Town.

Hours: daily 6:00-6:30 (some stall operators close at 6:00)
Tram: 6, 9, 18 or 22 to Národní Třída
Metro: Green ("A") line and Yellow ("B") line to Můstek

Old Town Square, Kampa Park (Na Kampě) and Ovocný Trh

Each of these squares originally served as marketplaces, and on special occasions or during certain seasons, each still does today. Old Town Square more often than not has some kind of market operating (such as an Easter market or a Christmas market, etc.). The quality, authenticity and desirability of the goods on offer vary from not bad or even interesting to kitschy. But the atmosphere can sometimes make up for this.

The food on offer is usually better than the souvenirs and other products. The "Prague Ham" that is roasting on open pits is especially good. But be aware that it is served by weight and the server will invariably pile a huge amount of meat on your paper plate and say, "OK?" You'll nod yes and then they'll quickly weigh it and you'll end up paying around $12 for a plate of street food. As I said, the ham is very good, but you can get a full meal with a beer in a pub for that amount of money. So, just be sure to watch how much ham they give you before you agree to have it weighed, at which point, there seems to be no turning back.

Markets are held less often on the Na Kampě square on Kampa Park (next to the Charles Bridge in Malá Strana) and on Ovocný Trh (behind the Estates Theater just off of Old Town square) and tend to be a bit more interesting and of better quality than the ones on Old Town Square when they do have them. **Around Bastille Day there usually is a very nice week-long French market on Kampa,** serving good wines and cheeses and other French delicacies.

In September you'll find **wine festivals ("vinobrani," or wine harvest),** and in the spring and autumn, there are beer festivals around town (usually at Prague Castle or on the embankment of the Vltava just south of Palackého Náměstí).

Hand-painted Easter eggs for sale at the Old Town Square Easter market

Farmer's Markets

The locavore trend began to infect Prague about two years ago. What started as one or two farmer's markets that were held only occasionally and then mostly in the warmer months has now turned into a network of markets to be found on almost every square (outside of the touristic center) almost year-round, several days a week. My locavore and fellow foodie friends all agree that the farmer's market at Náplavka is the best. It is probably the one you'll be most interested in, as well, as it is held along the picturesque river embankment on Saturday mornings, not too far from the center of town. The Náplavka market has a great atmosphere and food trucks with hot meals in addition to the farm fresh products. You can check the following link for more info on all of Prague's markets.

www.farmarsketrziste.cz/en

Note: as of this writing, the city authorities are attempting to move the Náplavka market further out of town. Let's hope not, but I will make an update if it does happen. In any case, check the website above before you go.

17 SHOPPING MALLS

I know – you probably don't want to go to a mall while you're in Prague. But not all malls are created equal, and a few of the malls in Prague have some unique features, so, just in case....

Palladium Shopping Center – on Náměstí Republiky

This mall is located in a former historical Austro-Hungarian army barracks, and the beautiful façade of the original building was left intact. On the lower floor, you will find excavated Romanesque ruins that were left exposed and incorporated into the building. The food court in this mall has some pretty good restaurants in addition to the usual fast food suspects. And, of course, the mall has restrooms (all on the uppermost/food court level or on the bottom level), free Wi-Fi at the Starbucks downstairs and at the McDonald's upstairs, and ATMs ("bankomat") sprinkled throughout.

Nový Smíchov Shopping Center (otherwise known as "Anděl" by locals) – at the Anděl tram and metro station in Smíchov

Like the Palladium, this mall was built on the site of a historical building (a factory in this case), whose rather attractive façade was left in place. The mall is pleasant enough, and has restrooms (only on the upper two levels), cash machines, a Tesco grocery store, a Marks & Spencer, cinemas and decent cafes. It also has a Česká Spořitelna Bank branch on the ground level that does foreign exchange.

Palladium shopping center at Christmas

18 SHOPPING STREETS

Some of these streets are mentioned elsewhere in this book, but since there are a couple of other streets in Prague that warrant a mention for the concentration of unique shopping they offer, I thought I would add a separate chapter here.

Pařížská Street

As has already been mentioned in the chapter titled "Luxury Shopping," this street is the premiere address when shopping for luxury brands.

Melantrichova, Karlova, Celetná, Nerudova and Mostecká Streets

These are the main paths of least resistance for tourist traffic, as they lead off of the Charles Bridge or Old Town Square or up to Prague Castle. Each is packed with all kinds of shops – mainly the junky souvenir kind. However, Nerudova, Melantrichova and Mostecká have some notable exceptions to this.

Havel's Market

You'll find this Old Town (and old) market covered in the chapter on "Outdoor Markets." It's a great place to shop for souvenirs and artwork and is located right at the end of Melantrichova Street.

Kavka bookshop on Karoliny Světlé

Karoliny Světlé

This street in Old Town is home to several unique shops, such as the Kavka bookshop featuring many interesting art book titles (mainly Czech). Another shop (Mar Len) is a real find for lovers of unique fabrics of all kinds. There's also a Czech bridal shop and a puppet shop called Czech Marionettes and listed in the chapter titled "Marionettes, Handicrafts and Toys." And when you finish shopping, you can have a drink at the famous Hemingway Bar.

Veverkova Street

The New York Times published an article on the shopping and dining opportunities found on this trendy street in Prague 7 titled *Five Places to Go in Prague* (Plockova, 2017). After shopping for books at Page Five, clothes or design items, you can have lunch or coffee at Cobra or Bistro 8.

Vinohradská Street

This grand avenue in the fashionable turn of the century (19th to 20th) Vinohrady neighborhood has become **the** locale for any serious home décor and design shop in Prague. See "Design, Specialty and Gift Shops."

Korunní

Korunní is another street in Vinohrady (which means "vineyards," as this is the place where the king used to have his vineyards on the area's southward sloping hills) that still has a dwindling number of antique, pawn and other unique shops on it (especially the first three or four blocks up from Náměstí Míru). You'll find a few decent eateries and interesting cafes here, as well.

Michalská

As was mentioned in "Art, Antiques and Collectibles," this street has a greater concentration of art galleries than most in Old Town, as does the passageway leading off the left-hand side of the northern end of it.

Chairs on display at Vinohradský Pavilon

19 SPORTS AND OUTDOORS

The Czechs are great outdoors people, and they especially love hiking and mountain climbing. In fact, the Czech forests are not only beautiful, but they are laced with some of the most well-marked and well-maintained hiking trails in the world. It's not surprising then that Prague has some great locally-owned and -run outdoor shops.

Hudy Sport

Hudy Sport was founded by professional climber Jindřich Hudeček, who was a member of the Czechoslovak mountaineering team from 1983 to 1990. Thanks to his close contacts with professionals in the sport, Hudeček's transition from professional climber to owner of an outdoor business after the Velvet Revolution of 1989 was easy.

In 1990, Hudeček founded a small outdoor equipment business that became the basis for Hudy Sport as it exists today (currently there are 39 retail outlets in the Czech and Slovak Republics). Most of the stores' employees are active climbers or athletes as well, so they can offer expert advice on your purchases.

The two Hudy locations that are in or closest to the center of town where you will likely be spending most of your time are:

Hudy Sport

Na Perštýně 14
Hours: Mon.-Fri. 10:00 – 19:30, Sat. 10:00 – 18:00, closed Sunday
Phone: 224 218 600
Tram: 2, 9, 18, 22 or 23 to Národní Třída
Metro: Yellow ("B") line to Národní Třída

Lidická 43
Hours: Mon.-Fri. 10:00 – 19:30, Sat. 10:00 – 18:00, closed Sunday
Phone: 257 315 964
Tram: 4, 5, 6, 7, 9, 10, 12, 15, 16, or 20 to Anděl
Metro: Yellow ("B") line to Anděl

Rock Point

Like Hudy, Rock Point was founded by a small group of nature enthusiasts who sought to *"bring inspiration and help others to rejoice in what they love - walking in nature."* The first shop selling the brands and types of equipment they used on their adventures was opened in 1997. Since then, the rest is history, and today Rock Point claims to be the number one place for everything related to the outdoors in Prague. In addition to hiking and climbing equipment, they offer advice and tailor-made recommendations.

There are currently 12 Rock Point locations in Prague. You can check their website for a full listing, but the ones you will probably be nearest are:

Rock Point

Na Poříčí 10
Hours: Mon.-Fri. 10:00 – 20:00, Sat.-Sun.10:00 – 18:00
Phone: 222 311 692
Tram: 6, 8, 15, 26 to Náměstí Republiky
Metro: Yellow ("B") line to Náměstí Republiky
www.rockpoint.cz/

Martinská 2
Hours: Mon.-Fri. 10:00-20:00, Sat.-Sun.10:00 – 18:00
Phone: 224 228 045
Tram: 2, 9, 18, 22 to Národní Třída
Metro: Yellow ("B") line to Národní Třída

20 TRAINS, PLANES AND AUTOMOBILES

The Czech Republic, like much of Central Europe and Germany in particular, has a fascination with model toys, especially model trains. And it has some great ones, as well as great shops that sell them. If you get to the outreaches of Prague, you'll find dozens of model shops, but here I will list just a few that are in or close to the center of town (and that are some of the city's best).

U Krále Železnic (At the Railroad King)

As the name proclaims, U Krále Železnic is the "Railroad King." This small shop is crammed with some of the most amazing and beautiful model train cars and engines that you'll find in one place. And it is crammed – every inch is filled with small shelves and showcases lined with the intricate models of just about every kind of train, old and new, domestic and international.

It's a couple of metro or tram stops out of the center of town, but not too far, and well worth the trip if you're a model train lover.

U Krále Železnic
Mánesova 42

Hours: Mon.-Fri. 11:00 – 18:00, Sat. 9:00 – 12:00
Phone: 222 25 25 25
Tram: 11 or 13 to Vinohradská tržnice
Metro: Green ("A") line to Jiřího z Poděbrad or Náměstí Míru
Email: ukralezeleznic@seznam.cz
www.ukralezeleznic.cz

U Krále Železnic trains

Království Autíček

Království Autíček (King of Cars) has over 10,000 model cars, motorcycles and aircraft from both internationally known manufacturers and small specialists. They also trade in second-hand models, so here you can find models and kits that have long since disappeared from sales counters elsewhere.

Království Autíček
Benediktská 9
Hours: Mon.-Fri. 10:00 – 18:00
Phone: 224 827 818
Email: objednavky@macmodel.cz

109

Tram: 6, 8, 15, or 26 to Dlouhá Třída
Bus: 207 to Dlouhá Třída
www.macmodel.cz

MPM Model Shop

In addition to model cars and trains, MPM also carries military vehicles and aircraft. And one thing I really love about it is that MPM also has models of local historic buildings and structures, such as the famous Charles Bridge. They also carry an extensive selection of adhesives and putty and other accessories for your model workshop.

MPM Model Shop
Myslíkova 19
Hours: Mon.-Fri. 9:00 – 18:00, Sat. 9:00 – 13:00, closed Sunday
Phone: 774 487 087
Tram: 5 to Myslíkova
www.mpmshop.eu

Railway Kingdom

Railway Kingdom is a family-friendly model railway museum featuring interactive and digitally-operated exhibits. It's located in the Smíchov neighborhood of Prague 5.

Railway Kingdom
Stroupežnického 23
Hours: daily 9:00 – 19:00
Phone: 257 211 386
Tram: 4, 5, 7, 9, 10, 12, 16, or 20 to Anděl
Metro: Yellow ("B") line to Anděl
www.railroad-kingdom.com/

Ben-Zerba

A favorite of locals, Ben-Zerba has one of largest product stocks in the Czech Republic. They also ship worldwide. Choose from cars, planes, trains, steam engines and more!

Ben-Zerba

Ostrovského 4

Hours: Mon. 13.00 – 18.00, Tue.-Fri. 10.00 – 18.00, Sat. 10.00 – 13.00

Phone: 257 213 625

Tram: 5, 12, or 20 to Na Knížecí

Metro: Yellow ("B") line to Anděl (exit Na Knížecí)

Email: info@ben-zerba.cz

www.ben-zerba.cz

21 TAX-FREE SHOPPING

Non-EU tourists in Prague are eligible for a refund of the VAT (value-added tax) of up to 21% on purchases over CZK 2,000. Look for stores with a "Tax Free Shopping" sign, and be sure to ask the clerk for a tax refund voucher when you make your purchase. You will then have to fill out some forms and present them along with the original receipts to an agent at Prague airport.

At the airport (Terminal 1 and Terminal 2), look for signs saying "Global Blue" or "Tax Refund." I believe the tax refund points are located **before** you go through passport control, so if you can't find them, **please be sure to ask before you pass through passport control** – otherwise you might miss your opportunity.

Note: Some shops in town offer to refund your credit card for your VAT amount at the time you purchase your goods. My advice is don't do it. The store will take a cut, and you still need to get a stamp at the airport anyway.

www.globalblue.com/tax-free-shopping/czech-republic

22 MONEY, CREDIT CARDS AND ATMS

The currency used here is the Czech crown ("koruna" in Czech), and at the time of this writing the exchange rate is around CZK 21 to US$1 (in the "good ol' days," you got 40 crowns for your dollar!) and approximately CZK 26 to the euro. **Be sure to check exchange rates before your trip**.

MONEY

You can, of course, exchange money at many of the exchange offices located throughout the city or at a bank. But, if you choose to go to an exchange office, **be sure to read the fine print before you change anything** – often the advertised rate is applicable only for very large amounts of money – much more than you would likely need on a holiday. Lesser amounts are changed at very disadvantageous rates. Actually, **most of these exchange offices really amount to a scam**. So, I prefer exchanging money at a bank.

If you plan to change money at a bank, note that you will not find bank branches open on the weekends, not even on a Saturday morning. Also, many bank branches close during lunchtime or early (1:00 or 4:00 PM) on certain days of the week. Check the hours posted outside or try to get there in the morning. In general, when you change money at a bank or exchange office, you will need to have your passport with you.

Note: If the bank is closed and you only want to use an ATM, you should be able to access some branch's ATMs by swiping your bankcard to gain access to the branch.

Many shops and restaurants accept euros, and the rates they give are not bad. But check the rate with your server or clerk before using this option. If you're not headed to the Eurozone after you leave Prague, you might want to get rid of your euros this way, especially if you would otherwise have to exchange more money for crowns anyway.

If someone approaches you on the street and asks if you want to "change money," **DO NOT DO IT**. It's a scam, and you will walk away with a rolled up wad of worthless Belorussian or other currency hidden behind a CZK 100 note (worth about $5).

ATMS

You can also use your normal bank, debit or credit cards at ATMs ("bankomat" in Czech). Just be aware that the fee for each withdrawal at a bankomat is US$5, plus a percentage of the amount withdrawn, so be careful about the frequency of withdrawals and associated fees.

ATMs offer an "English" option on the first screen under languages. Some might detect your card's bank and automatically switch to English. On their default screens, most ATMs offer a maximum withdrawal of CZK 4,000 (about US$200). However, you may opt out of selecting a default amount by hitting the "Other Amount" option. This way you can withdraw more than the default amount in order to avoid multiple withdrawals. Just be sure you've done a quick conversion into U.S. dollars or your currency of the Czech amount you intend to withdraw so that you don't inadvertently exceed your card's limit and get your card blocked by your bank.

In recent years, some "no-name" ATMs have appeared in the tourist areas of town. Many of my clients have used them, and I have not heard of any problems. However, I have noticed that the default withdrawal amounts start at HUGE sums. And with visitors not being familiar with the currency and conversion rates and perhaps being in a rush, will automatically select the amount at the top of the screen (which is the smallest amount on the screen) without thinking about it. And they probably withdrew about $1000 when they meant to take out $100 or $200. So if you use one of these, take care when selecting the withdrawal amount.

Many ATMs (and credit card terminals also) now offer a new option when making withdrawals with a bank card from a foreign bank: "Accept with Conversion" or "Accept without Conversion." I use "without," as the option "with" seems to use an even worse exchange rate. The credit card terminals at some shops and restaurants also offer this option now, so pay attention. Also, some employees will not ask you and will select "with conversion" for you without your knowledge. So you might want to mention ahead of time that you want to pay in Czech crowns.

Here are a few ATM/bankomat locations to save you time looking, as they're not so easy to find in the old city center:

- Palladium Shopping Center on Náměstí Republiky (several machines near the front and side entrances and on the lower level). Take the yellow or "B" metro line or trams 6, 8, 15 and 26 to Náměstí Republiky,
- IP Pavlova and Náměstí Republiky metro stations,
- Česká Spořitelna Bank at the corner of Rytířská and Melantrichova Streets,
- Mostecká Street and Malostranské Náměstí in Malá Strana.

And here is a list of some bank branches where you can change money:

- Česká Spořitelna bank branches: at the corner of Rytířská and Melantrichova Streets in Old Town, on Mostecká Street in Malá Strana and in the Anděl shopping mall at

the Anděl metro and tram stop,
* ČSOB bank branch on Náměstí Republiky (which also
  has ATMs inside).

**If you have large bills (which in Prague means a CZK
1,000 note or larger)** and try to buy something for a much smaller
amount, expect to have trouble changing it (especially with taxis).
You will almost surely be met with "Nemáte menší?" ("Don't you
have anything smaller?"), and some places will flat out refuse to
accept your money or sell you anything! Many shops and vendors
seem to be fine with losing a sale over this. So, if you get large bills
at a cash machine (and cash machines will almost always give you
large bills!), try to change them as soon as you can, like when
paying for a more pricey item or a meal for several people. And
hold onto your small bills and coins for use at cafes and restrooms
or markets or for buying tram tickets or post cards, etc.

If you do change money at a bank, ask them for smaller bills
and maybe they will accommodate your request. Thankfully, some
ATMs now offer an option where you can choose the
denomination of your bills, but CZK 1,000 is usually the smallest
on offer if you withdraw a larger amount (which you'll want to do
in order to have fewer withdrawals and therefore fewer $5
withdrawal fees as mentioned before, and because CZK 1,000 is
only about $50!).

Here's a tip: If you're stuck with large bills and can't seem to get
change, go to McDonald's or Starbucks and buy something small –
just to get change. They are the only places that are almost certain
not to give you a hard time – they won't even ask you if you have
something smaller – what service! They will simply change it for
you. McDonald's requires you to buy something, though.
Starbucks might do it without a purchase if you ask nicely, but I
can't guarantee that. Note that in nicer restaurants, paying with
larger bills shouldn't be a problem.

CREDIT CARDS

Most restaurants and shops in Prague accept major credit cards
these days. MasterCard, Visa and Diners are the most widely-

accepted, while most places don't take American Express (many hotels and finer restaurants are the exceptions). Using credit cards is more convenient than dealing with ATMs and cash. Therefore, I would use this option where possible. But be aware that most credit cards issued in the U.S. will charge a "foreign transaction fee" on purchases you make abroad. And though Europe is moving to chip/PIN cards, you should have no trouble with cards that need to be swiped or with chip/sign.

In general, I would advise you to be sure to check the amount being charged before signing or entering your PIN for a credit card transaction. There have been incidents of credit card fraud in the past. While I have heard of this happening, I personally have never had any problem with using a credit card in Prague. Even so, I would advise paying cash in the junkier souvenir shops to be on the safe side. But at most places listed in this book, it should be OK.

23 CONTACT ME

Thank you for purchasing my Prague Shopping Guide! I hope you will find it helpful in leading you to some great shopping experiences. In addition to this and my other guidebooks, I also offer the following services:

Private Guided Tours – Your Interests, Your Pace

For almost a decade, I've provided private guided tours of Prague to discerning travelers of all stripes and ages. My tours are tailored to your interests and pace, and in addition to showing you the most significant historical sites of this city, I'll point out the best places to eat and shop, and I will also show you how to get around on your own. On my tours, we'll get off the beaten path as much as possible, helping you see the "real" Prague, and my aim will be to help you make the most of your time here.

I'd be delighted to meet you and give you a personal introduction to this city that I still find amazing after all of these years. And I can also take you on a shopping tour if you like!

Day Trips – Kutná Hora

I also offer day trips to the historical UNESCO town of Kutná Hora should you be interested in exploring the Czech Republic beyond Prague. Kutná Hora is a beautiful, mostly Gothic, city, with many historical landmarks revealing its rich silver mining past. It is one of my favorite places to visit and is highly recommended. In addition to the historical structures, the town itself offers stunning views of its small valley from the "hora" (small mountain). Kutná Hora also has a wonderful art gallery and a great, very local place to have lunch.

So, if you're interested in a private guided tour, please contact me at: krysti.brice@seznam.cz or through my website at: www.exclusivepraguetours.com.

Kutná Hora

Concierge Services – Make the Most of Your Time in Prague

In any foreign country, making arrangements and plans can be a challenge. And in the Czech Republic, given the difficulty of the Czech language and the not-always-helpful or forthcoming customer service, it can be downright daunting. Under my

"Concierge Services," I offer travel advice and assistance, saving you time, energy – and perhaps money, too.

As I mentioned in the chapter on Czech history, the quality of classical music and opera here is outstanding – and quite affordable, too. Not only that, but the venues are spectacular and historic as well (and you might recognize a few interiors from movies you've watched in your home country). Researching and purchasing tickets to concerts during your visit is a task that I perform for clients often under my Concierge Services. I am also familiar with the seating and acoustics in most of the venues, so I can help you get the best experience for your money.

When it comes to train travel, several interesting destinations are easily reached by daily trains from Prague, including:

- Berlin
- Dresden
- Vienna
- Budapest.

If you want help with train schedules and purchasing tickets, I can do that for you. I can also explain the workings of Prague's train station, how to find your track, etc. Often the prices of tickets purchased here in advance are slightly cheaper than what you'll pay if you buy them online outside of the Czech Republic, especially when it comes to international destinations.

So, if you want help getting concert or train information, buying tickets or making reservations at some of the best restaurants in Prague, I can do all that for you and save you time and energy spent surfing the web. Click here for more details which can be found on my website:

www.exclusivepraguetours.com/concierge

My Unique Prague Guidebook

If you want more information on Prague, including sightseeing tips and practical information about things like public transportation and restrooms, my guidebook is just the thing for you! It's available in paperback and for Kindle and other digital devices (smartphones and tablets) through my website or on Amazon.com.

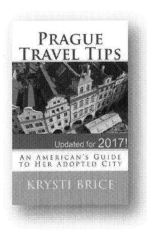

My Prague Restaurant Guide

In addition to being an art, architecture and history lover, I'm also a major foodie. That means that I really suffered in the early years after moving here, when you couldn't even get orange juice! "Real" cappuccino or good wine? Fuggedaboutit! But I guess good things really do come to those who wait, and now Prague is a European food capital (no kidding). So naturally I wrote a book about it.

And don't worry about all the calories you'll consume when you indulge in the delicious Czech beer and roasted duck on offer. You'll walk it all off on one of my tours!

Self-Guided Walks

If you prefer to explore a new city on your own, my self-guided walks will help you do just that! Wander through Prague's significant historical areas and learn about its history and landmarks. These walks contain maps and photos, and even if you do take a tour with me, they are great for helping you sort through your photos when you get home.

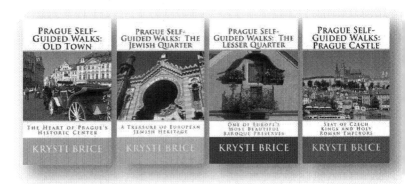

Recommended Travel Accessories

After many years traveling the globe with the World Bank and many subsequent years as a guide for visitors to the Czech

Republic, I've gained a lot of knowledge about the accessories you need on the road, which ones are hard (or impossible) to find here, etc., including some you might not have thought of. Before you travel, take a look at the recommendations on my website:

www.exclusivepraguetours.com/electronics-travel-accessories

Portable charger

Recommended Reading

And in addition to recommended travel accessories, I also have a list of some great titles for you to read before your trip to Prague. Get the most out of your time and experience in the Czech Republic by immersing yourself in Czech culture and history before you arrive.

www.exclusivepraguetours.com/books-by-czech-authors

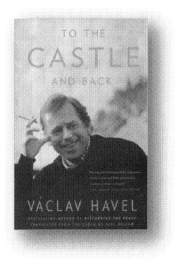

Facebook and More

And finally, if you're on Facebook, check out my Tour Page to see great photos of Prague and get up-to-date information on what's going on in the city. And I would love it if you would "Like" my page:

www.facebook.com/ExclusivePragueTours.

Thanks, and I wish you a great time in Prague!

Krysti

24 LIST OF SHOPS BY NEIGHBORHOOD

OLD TOWN

Antik v Dlouhé (Antiques on Dlouhá)
Antikvariát & Galerie
Antikvariát Valentinská
Artěl (also in Malá Strana)
AD Galerie on Uhelný Trh
Blue (also in Malá Strana)
Bohemia Paper (J Orb Paper Shop)
Bořek Šípek
Bric a Brac
Botanicus
Country Life (and other locations)
Czech Marionettes
Dorotheum
Erpet Bohemia Crystal
Fajans Majolica (Ceramic Workshop of Juraj Vanya)
Flying Tiger (and other locations)
Food Story
The Franz Kafka Society
Galerie Art Praha
Galerie Jakubska
Gourmet Pasáž Dlouhá

Havel's Market (Havelské tržiště)
Hefaistos
Hračky u Zlatého Lva
Hudební Nástroje Radek Bubrle
Hudební Nástroje "U Zlatého Kohouta"
Hudy Sport (and other locations)
Království Autiček
Kubista
La Bodeguita del Medio
La Bottega
La Casa del Argentina
Le Patio (also in New Town)
Lípa
Manufaktura (also in Malá Strana)
Material
Moser (also in New Town)
National Marionette Theater
Organic and Natural Cosmetics
Pod 7 Kilo (Under 7 Kilos)
Pařížská Street (Luxury Shopping)
Preciosa
Rock Point (and other locations)
Turnov Granát
Via Musica
V Ungeltu
Zlatá Loď

MALÁ STRANA

AleAle
AMI Loutky - Obchod Loutkami
Hunter-Just Your Friend
Koh-i-Noor (and New Town)
Manufaktura (and Old Town)
Potten & Pannen
Shakespeare & Sons Bookshop
Truhlář Marionety
Vetešnictví

NEW TOWN

Albert (and other locations)
Baťa
Billa (and other locations)
DelMart (and other locations)
FotoŠkoda
Dr. Hauschka
The Globe Bookshop
Happyfeet Vinyl Record Shop Prague
Jaroslava (Women's Fashion)
Koh-i-Noor (and Malá Strana)
Marks & Spencer (and other locations)
Moser (and Old Town)
MPM Model Shop
Naoko 1 & 2
NeoLuxor (and in other locations)
Palladium Shopping Center
Papelote
Phono.cz
Tesco/My (and other locations)

VINOHRADY

Book Therapy
Dům Porcelánu
Houslařský Atelier Vávra
Moleskin
U Krále Železnic (At the Railroad King)
Vinohradský Pavilon
Zastavárna on Korunní

SMÍICHOV

Ben-Zerba
Nový Smíchov Shopping Center
Railway Kingdom
Tesco

WineFoodMarket

HRADČANY (PRAGUE CASTLE DISTRICT)

Christmas Shop at Prague Castle
Hračky – Houpací Kůň (The Rocking Horse Toy Shop)

25 LIST OF SHOPS BY CATEGORY

Crystal, Fine Glass and Porcelain

Artěl Malá Strana
Bořek Šípek
Dům Porcelánu
Erpet
Material
Moser
Preciosa

Garnets and Other Jewelry, Clothing and Shoes

AleAle
Bat'a
Erpet
Turnov Granát
Jaroslava (Women's Fashion)

Marionettes, Handicrafts, and Toys

AMI Loutky (Marionettes)

Botanicus
Czech Marionettes
Fajans Majolica (Ceramic Workshop of Juraj Vanya)
Hračky – Houpací Kůň (The Rocking Horse Toy Shop)
Hračky u Zlatého Lva (Toys)
Manufaktura
National Marionette Theater
Truhlář Marionety
V Ungeltu

Souvenirs

Blue

Art, Antiques and Collectibles

AD Galerie
Antik v Dlouhé
Bric a Brac
Dorotheum
Gallerie Art Praha
Galerie Jakubska
Koh-i-noor Stationary
Vetešnictví
Zastavárna on Korunní
Zlatá Loď

Books and Antiquarian shops

Antikvariát & Galerie
Antikvariát Valentinská
Book Therapy
The Franz Kafka Society
The Globe
NeoLuxor
Shakespeare & Sons

Design, Specialty and Gift Shops

Bohemia Paper (J. Orb Paper Shop)
Christmas Shop at Prague Castle
Flying Tiger
FotoŠkoda
Hefaistos
Hunter-Just Your Friend
Kubista
La Bodeguita del Medio
La Casa del Argentina
Lípa
Moleskin
Naoko 1 & 2
Papelote
Pod 7 Kilo (Under 7 Kilos)
Vinohradský Pavilon

Gourmet Food Shops and Grocery Stores

Albert
Billa
DelMart
Food Story
Gourmet Pasáž Dlouhá
La Bottega
Marks & Spencer
Tesco
WineFood Market

Health and Beauty

Botanicus
Country Life
Dr. Hauschka
Organic and Natural Cosmetics

Home, Housewares and Kitchen

Le Patio
Potten & Pannen

Luxury Shopping

Tiffany
Hermes
Louis Vuitton
Cartier
Prada
Gucci and more…

Music and Musical Instruments

Happyfeet Vinyl Record Shop Prague
Houslařský Atelier Vávra (Vávra Violin Studio)
Hudební Nástroje Radek Bubrle (Musical Instruments)
Hudební Nástroje "U Zlatého Kohouta" (Musical Instruments)
Phono.cz
Via Musica

Outdoor Markets

Havel's Market (Havelské Tržíště)
Old Town Square, Kampa Park (Na Kampě) and Ovocný Trh
Farmer's Markets

Shopping Malls

Anděl (Nový Smíchov Shopping Center)
Palladium

Shopping Streets

Havel's Market (Havelské Tržíště)
Karoliny Světlé
Korunní
Melantrichova, Karlova, Celetná, Nerudova and Mostecká Streets
Michalská
Pařížská Street
Veverkova Street
Vinohradská Street

Sports and Outdoors

Hudy
Rock Point

Trains, Planes and Automobiles

Ben-Zerba
Království Autíček
MPM Model Shop
Railway Kingdom
U Krále Železnic

26 MAPS

Map 1: General overview of Prague

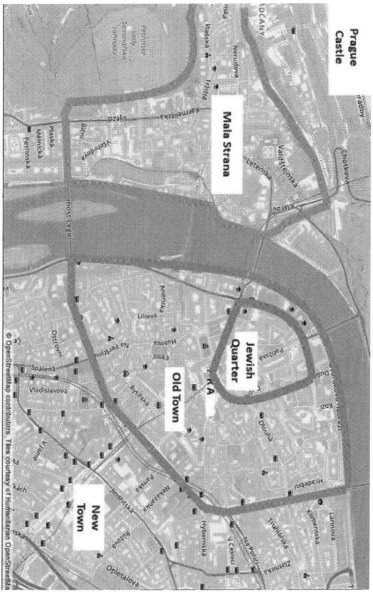

© 2018 OpenStreetMap Contributors and Krysti Brice

Map 2: Old Town Map

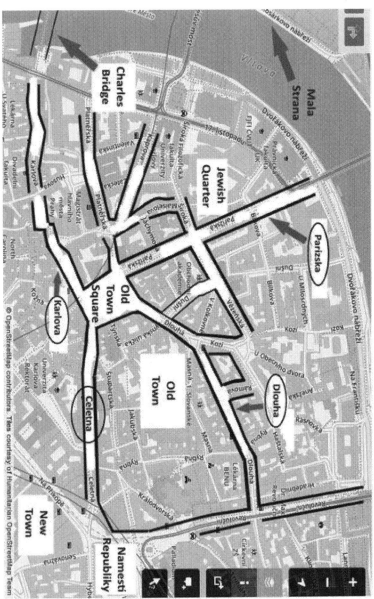

Map 3: Malá Strana Map

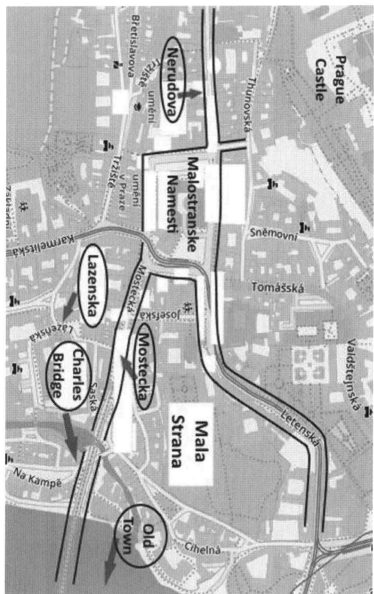

© 2018 OpenStreetMap Contributors and Krysti Brice

Map 4: Vinohrady Map

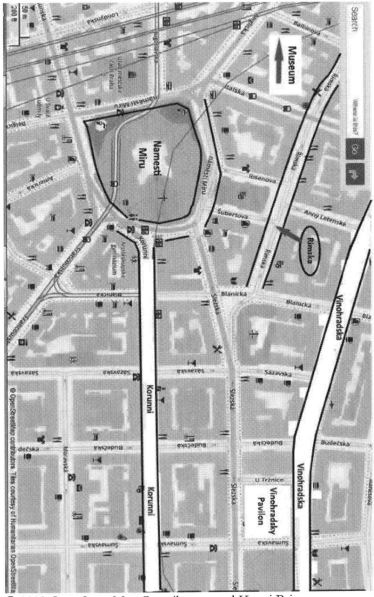

ABOUT THE AUTHOR

Krysti Brice, a native of Macon, Georgia, and a graduate of New York University, is a former CPA and investment banker who began her career at Deloitte in New York City. In 1992, she moved to Prague where she continued her work at Deloitte as an adviser to the Ministry of Privatization. While in Prague, she joined the World Bank and was based in both Prague and Washington, DC. After her last tour of duty in Washington ended in 2000, she returned to Prague, where she now works as an author, mentor and guide to the city.

Made in the USA
San Bernardino, CA
22 April 2019

Erpet

As mentioned in the chapter on crystal, this shop on Old Town Square also carries Czech garnets. The garnets in the front of the store are mined in Turnov, whereas the room off the back of the store that also contains Czech porcelain has garnets mined both in Turnov and in another mine that yields even darker stones.

Between the two in the center of the store you'll also find amber. Erpet has some beautiful amber pieces, but keep in mind that, generally, most amber for sale in Prague is not usually from the Czech Republic. Most likely it is from Poland. Moldevite is a beautiful green stone that is mined locally, and Erpet has jewelry set with this stone, sometimes accompanied by diamonds, in the front of the store.

Erpet interior – photo reprinted with the permission of Erpet Group a.s.

As you walk around Prague, you'll notice that garnet shops are almost as ubiquitous as crystal shops. Years ago there were only a few shops specializing in garnet jewelry, and those original shops were all quite reliable. But included in the new explosion of garnet shops are many rip-off places selling fakes. My advice is to stay away from them and shop for garnets at Erpet or the other shop listed below. Erpet provides a certificate of authentication with all of the garnet jewelry it sells.

Erpet Bohemia Crystal

Old Town Square 27
Hours: daily 10:00 – 23:00
Phone: 224 229 755, 224 229 755
Tram: 2, 17 or 18 to Staroměstská
Metro: Green ("A") line to Staroměstská, or green ("A") and yellow ("B") line to Můstek
Email: info@erpetcrystal.cz
www.erpetcrystal.cz

The other good shop for garnets is Turnov Granát:

Turnov Granát

Dlouhá 28
Hours: Mon.-Sat. 9:00 – 19:00, Sun. 10:00 – 17:00
Phone: 222 315 612
Tram: 6, 8, 15, or 26 to Dlouhá Třída
Bus: 207 to Dlouhá Třída

AleAle

It's hard to describe with words just how beautiful and special the glass bead jewelry pieces made by this local artist are. And each piece by Alena Chládková is unique – the artist never copies the exact same design or motif – so whatever you take home will be one of a kind. And the prices are incredibly reasonable considering the amount of work that goes into each piece. Alena's work is so good that it was featured in British *Vogue* a few years back. She has two shops in Prague (both in the Malá Strana) showcasing her necklaces, bracelets, earrings and more. The main location is listed here:

AleAle

Lázeňská 2
Hours: Mon.-Sat.10:30-18:30, closed Sunday

Phone: Not listed
Tram: 12, 15, 20, 22 or 23 to Hellichova
Email: aleale@aleale.cz
www.aleale.cz

Baťa

Baťa is a world-famous Czech brand of shoes originally manufactured in the Czech Republic – well, famous just about everywhere in the world except the US (I'm not sure why, but I'm sure there's an interesting story behind that fact). Founded in the town of Zlín in the Moravian region of the Czech Republic by Tomáš Baťa in 1894, the company now boasts more than 5,000 retail stores. Tomáš Baťa himself is legendary for being a visionary business leader (he is sometimes called "the Henry Ford of Europe"), and the remnants of his workers' village in Zlín have now become trendy, highly-sought-after retro housing.

Baťa shoes are both stylish and affordable, and like Baťa's workers' village, the company's flagship store in Prague on Wenceslas Square (Václavské Náměstí) is also noteworthy for its ahead-of-its-time 1920's Functionalist design.

Baťa

Václavské Náměstí 6
Hours: Mon.-Sat. 9:00 – 21:00; Sun. 10:00 – 21:00
Phone: 221 088 478
Tram: 3, 5, 6, 9, 14, 24 to Václavské Náměstí
Metro: Green ("A") line or Yellow ("B") line to Můstek
www.bata.cz

Jaroslava – Design by Jaroslava Procházková

Jaroslava Procházková is one of the most popular and successful Czech fashion designers, and her signature women's knitwear is marked by timeless style, unique and sophisticated color combinations and quality workmanship, (custom tailoring is part of her shop's service). Jaroslava is located in the Lucerna Pasáž, which is itself worth a visit to see its stunning original Art Nouveau interior, as well as a famous (equestrian, of sorts) work by the Czech contemporary artist, David Černý.

Jaroslava – Design by Jaroslava Procházková
Vodičkova 36
Hours: Not listed
Phone: 731 483 847
Tram: 3, 5, 6, 9, 14, 24 to Václavské Náměstí
Metro: Green ("A") line or Yellow ("B") line to Můstek (exit to Vodičkova Street)
www.jaroslava.cz/en

Otherwise, when it comes to **Czech fashion and Czech designers**, it would be worth your while wandering around the area of Old Town **bordered by Dlouhá, Dušní, Vězenská and Rámová Streets.** It's also a nice area of town to wander around, as it's not completely inundated with tourists and tourist shops – yet.